READY RECKONER *for* INDIAN ECONOMY

Third Edition

Madhur M. Mahajan
Assistant Professor, PG Dept. of Economics,
GGDSD College, Chandigarh
(Affiliated to Panjab University, Chandigarh)

***This Ready Reckoner is a component of the Third Edition of Indian Economy (ISBN: 9789361595554) and is not available for individual sale.**

Pearson

PREFACE

This Ready Reckoner is a crucial component of the third edition of Indian Economy (ISBN: 9789361595554). It has been designed to provide students with quick access to precise and reliable information, eliminating the need to conduct random Internet searches through unverified websites and sources. The reckoner encompasses a range of essential materials, including key statistics about India, a detailed commentary on the economic survey, budget, and multiple choice questions along with the answer keys based on the chapters of the main book. This resource aims to streamline the study process by consolidating critical information and offering clear, validated answers to support students' learning and understanding of the subject matter.

Madhur M. Mahajan

Table of Contents

UNIT I
STATISTICS OF INDIA

For a vast and diverse country like India, statistics is key to decision–making by various stakeholders like government institutions, public and private organizations, etc., for delivering, distributing and consuming products and services. It also reflects trends about resource delegation decisions by businesses, governments and various other groups and communities make. These statistics play an important role in understanding, interpreting, and analysing economic data such as the relationship between the quantity and price, supply and demand, economic output, per capita income of nations, GDP, etc.

1. Area of India

Total Area	3287263 Sq. Km
Percentage of World Area	2.42% (7th place in the world followed by Russia, Canada, The United States, China, Australia, and Brazil
Coast line	7516.6 Km (Mainland, Lakshadweep, Andaman and Nicobar Islands)
Continental shelf	0.53 million sq. Km
Forest and Tree cover area (2021)	809537 Sq. Km (24.62% of total area)
Total Forest Cover Area (2021)	713789 Sq. Km (21.71% of total geographical area)
Agriculture Land	179.993 million hectares
Arable Land	153.672 million hectares
Net sown area	139.902 million hectares
Per capita agriculture land	0.135 hectares
Gross irrigated area	112.23 million hectares
Net irrigated area	74.46 million hectares
Rainfed area as a percentage of net sown area	46.9%
Largest state	Rajasthan
Smallest state	Goa
State sharing boundaries with maximum states	Uttar Pradesh—State boundaries touched are Uttarakhand, Himachal, Haryana, Rajasthan, Madhya Pradesh

2. Population Statistics

Total Population of the country (2011 census)	**121.0854 crore**
Total Population of the country (RBI, 2022–23)	**138.29 crore**
Total Population of the country (World Population Review, 10 May, 2024)	**144.98 crore**
Decadal Growth Rate	17.7%
Percentage of World Population (2011)	17.5%
Total Rural Population (2011)	83.37 crore
Rural Population Growth	12.3%
Total Urban Population (2011)	37.71 crore
Urban Population Growth	31.8%
Sex ratio (2011)	943
Sex Ratio ((females per 1,000 males) as per NFHS–5 (2020–21)	1020
Birth Rate (2020)	19.5
Death Rate	6
Population below age 15 years NFHS–5 (2020–21)	26.5%

Total Fertility Rate (children per woman)	2.0
Infant Mortality Rate (IMR) (per 1,000 live births)	35.2
Institutional Births (%)	88.6%
Female Literacy (2019–21)	71.5%
Male Literacy (2019–21)	84.4%
Maternal Mortality Rate (per 100000 live births) (2018–20)	97
Life Expectancy at Birth (2022)	67.7

3. National Income (in ₹)

GVA at Basic Prices (2011–12 prices)	**1,38,76,840 (2021-22)** **1,48,04,901 (2022-23)** **1,58,27,708 (2023-24)**
GVA growth rate (2011–12 prices)	6.7% (2022–23) 6.9% (2023–24)
Per capita GDP (2011–12 prices)	1,16,216 (2022–23) 1,23,945 (2023–24)
GVA at Basic Prices (Current Prices)	2,16,35,584 (2021–22) 2,46,59,041 (2022–23) 2,66,77,679 (2023–24)
GVA growth rate (Current Prices)	14% (2022–23) 8.2 (2023–24)
Per capita GDP (Current prices)	1,72,422 (2021–22) 1,94,879 (2022–23) 2,10,679 (2023–24)

4. National Income Estimates – Sector Wise 2023–24 (First Advanced Estimates)

Industry	At Current Prices	At Constant Prices (2011–12)
Agriculture, Forestry & Fishing	5.5%	1.8%
Primary Sector	5.5	1.8
Mining & Quarrying	5.8	8.1
Manufacturing	4.4	6.5
Electricity, Gas & Water Supply and other Utility Services	9.2	8.3
Construction	9.6	10.7
Secondary Sector	6.5	7.9
Trade, Hotels, Transport, Communication & Services related to Broadcasting	5.8	6.3
Financial, Rear Estate & other financial Services	9.9	8.9
Public Administration, Defence & other Services	13.8	7.7
Tertiary Services	9.6	7.7
GVA at Basic Prices	8.0	6.9

5. Saving and Capital Formation

Gross Saving	₹73.63 lakh crore (2021–22) ₹81.50 lakh crore (2022–23)
Share of Non–financial corporations	37.3% (2022–23)
Share of Financial corporations	9.3% (2022–23)
Share of General Government	(–) 7.5% (2022–23)
Share of Household sectors	60.9% (2022–23)
Rate of Gross Saving to Gross National	30.8 (2021–22)
Disposable Income (GNDI)	29.7 (2022–23)
Gross Capital Formation (GCF)	₹76.48 lakh crore (2021–22) ₹86.78 lakh crore (2022–23)
Rate of GCF to GDP	32.4 (2021–22) 32.2 (2022–23)
Rate of GCF to GDP at constant (2011–12) prices	36.7% (2021–22) 34.9% (2022–23)

6. Annual Growth rate of GDP (at constant prices)

First Plan 1951–56	**3.6%**
Second Plan 1956–61	4.1%
Third Plan 1961–66	2.5%
Three Annual Plans (Plan Holiday) 1966–69	3.8%
Fourth Plan 1969–74	3.3%
Fifth Plan 1974–79	5%
Annual Plan 1979–80	6%
Sixth Plan 1980–85	5.4%
Seventh Plan 1985–90	5.8%
Annual Plan 1990–92	3%
Eighth Plan 1992–97	6.7%
Ninth Plan 1997–2002	5.5%
Tenth Plan 2002–07	7.8%
Eleventh Plan 2007–12	7.9%
Twelfth Plan 2012–17	6.8%
2016–17	8.2%
2017–18	7.2%
2018–19	6.5%
2019–20	4%
2020–21	–6.6%
2021–22	9.1%
2022–23	7.2%
2023–24	7.3%

7. India Human Development Indicators

Human Development Index (2022)	
India's Rank	134 out of 193 countries.
India's HDI value	0.644
Best performer in the world	Switzerland (Rank 1)
Worst performer in the world	Somalia (Rank 193)
Multi–dimensional Poverty Index (2023)	Incidence of poverty 2005/06: 55.1% (645 million) 2019/21: 16.4% (230 million)
Gender Development Index (2022)	
GDI Value for India	0.852
Female HDI Value for India	0.582
Male HDI Value for India	0.684
Gender Inequality Index (2022)	
India's Rank	108 out of 193 countries
World Happiness Index (2024)	
India Rank	126 (out of 143 nations)
India's Happiness Index Score	4.054
Best performer in the world	Finland (Rank 1)
Worst performer in the world	Afghanistan (Rank 143)
Poverty in India	
World Bank Estimates ($2.15 per day)	21.2% of population in 2011 12.92% of population in 2021
Poverty Headcount Ratio as per National Multidimensional Poverty Index	2005–06 55.34 2015–16 24.85 2022–23 11.28
Poorest State in India (2022–23)	Bihar (26.59)
Least Poor State in India (2022–23)	Goa (0.37)

8. Employment Statistics: 2022–23

Usual status, aged 15 years and above	
LFPR	57.9%
WPR	56%
UR	3.2%
State with highest unemployment	Goa (9.7)
State with least unemployment	Tripura (1.4)
Current Weekly status, aged 15 years and above	
LFPR	54.6
WPR	51.8
UR	5.1
Distribution of workers by broad industry divisions	
Agriculture	45.8
Manufacturing	11.4
Construction	13.0
Trade, Hotel & Restaurant	12.1
Transport, Storage & Communication	5.4
Other services	11.4
Trend in broad category wise employment status	
Self employed	57.3
Regular wage/salary	20.9
Casual labour	21.8

(Contd.)

Share of female workforce in self-employment	
Rural Female	
Own account worker and employer	27.9
Helper in household enterprise	43.1
Urban Female	
Own account worker and employer	27.6
Helper in household enterprise	40.4
Youth employment indicators	
LFPR	44.5
WPR	40.1
UR	10.0
Rural India Female LFPR	41.5
Urban India Female LFPR	25.4
All India Female LFPR	37.0
Top six states in terms of number of factories	Tamil Nadu, Gujarat, Maharashtra, Uttar Pradesh, Karnataka, Haryana
Top six states in terms of number of employment	Tamil Nadu, Gujarat, Maharashtra, Uttar Pradesh, Karnataka, Haryana

9. Agriculture Statistics - Production in Million Tonnes

Crop	2022–23 (Final)	2023–24 (First Advanced Estimates)
Rice	135.76	106.31
Wheat	110.55	–
Bazra	11.17	9.43
Maize	38.08	22.48
Coarse Cereals	57.32	35.13
Pulses	26.06	–
Total Foodgrains	329.69	–
Total Oilseeds	41.36	–
Cotton In Lacs bales (Bales = 170 kg)	33.67	31.65
Jute & Mesta In Lacs bales (Bales = 180 kg)	9.39	9.19
Sugarcane	490.53	434.80

10. State wise Agriculture Data

Top Wheat Producer State in India	Uttar Pradesh
Top Rice Producer State in India	West Bengal
Top Pulses Producer State in India	Madhya Pradesh
Top Coarse Cereals Producer State in India	Karnataka
Top Oilseeds Producer State in India	Rajasthan
Top Sugarcane Producer State in India	Uttar Pradesh
Top Jute & Mesta Producer State in India	West Bengal
Top Maize Producer State in India	Karnataka
Top Gram Producer State in India	Maharashtra
Top Groundnut Producer State in India	Gujarat

11. Minimum Support Price (₹ per quintal)

Sl. No.	Commodity	2021–22	2022–23	2023–24
	KHARIF CROPS			
1	Paddy common	1940	2040	2183
	Grade 'A'	1960	2060	2203
2	Jowar Hybrid	2738	2970	3180
	Maldandi	2758	2990	3225
3	Bajra	2250	2350	2500
4	Ragi	3377	3578	3846
5	Maize	1870	1962	2090
6	Tur (arhar)	6300	6600	7000
7	Moong	7275	7755	8558
8	Urad	6300	6600	6950
9	Groundnut	5550	5850	6377
10	Sunflower Seed	6015	6400	6760
11	Soyabeen (yellow)	3950	4300	4600
12	Sesamum	7307	7830	8635
13	Nigerseed	6930	7287	7734
14	Cotton			
	Medium Staple	5726	6080	6620
	Long Staple	6025	6380	7020
	RABI CROPS			
15	Wheat	2015	2125	2275
16	Barley	1635	1735	1850
17	Gram	5230	5335	5440
18	Masur (lentil)	5500	6000	6425
19	Rapeseed & Mustard	5050	5450	5650
20	Safflower	5441	5650	5800
	Other crops			
21	Copra (calendar Year) Milling	10335	10590	10860
	Ball	10600	11000	11750
22	Jute	4500	4750	5050

12. Banking Statistics

Establishment of RBI	April 1, 1935
RBI Headquarter	Mumbai
Nationalization of RBI	1949
Governor of RBI	Shri Shaktikanta Das
Number of Public Sector Banks	12 State Bank of India, Punjab National Bank, Bank of Baroda, Canara Bank, Union Bank of India, Bank of India, Indian Bank, Central Bank of India, Indian Overseas Bank, UCO Bank, Bank of Maharashtra, Punjab & Sindh Bank

(Contd.)

Number of Private Sector Banks	21
Number of Foreign Banks in India	44
Number of Regional Rural Banks	43
Number of Payment Banks	6
Number of Small Finance Banks	11
Number of Local Area Banks	2
Number of State Co–operative Banks	34
Policy rates, Reserve Ratios & Call Rates (as on 23rd May, 2024)	
Policy Repo Rate	6.50%
Standing Deposit Facility Rate	6.25%
Marginal Standing Facility Rate	6.75%
Bank Rate	6.75%
Fixed Reverse Repo Rate	3.35%
CRR	4.50%
SLR	18.00%
Base Rate	9.10% – 10.25%
MCLR (Overnight)	8.00% – 8.60%
Savings Deposit Rate	2.70% – 3.00%
Term Deposit Rate > 1 Year	6.00% – 7.25%
Call Rates	5.10% – 6.85%

13. Foreign Exchange Reserves (as on May 5, 2024)

Particulars	US $ Billion
Foreign Exchange Reserves (i+ii+iii+iv)	641.59
i. Foreign Currency Assets (FCA)	564.16
ii. Gold	54.88
iii. Special Drawing Rights (SDRs)	18.05
iv. Reserve Tranche Position (RTP)	4.50

14. FDI Statistics

Cumulative Amount of FDI Inflow (Equity inflow + 'Re–invested earnings' +'Other capital') from April, 2000 to December, 2023	USD 9,71,521 Million
Total FDI Inflow (April 2022–March 2023)	USD Million 46,034
Top 5 sectors attracting highest FDI (April 2022–March 2023)	Services Sector, Computer Software & Hardware, Trading, Telecommunications, Automobile Industry
Top 5 States/UTs Attracting Highest FDI Equity Inflow (April 2022–March 2023)	Maharashtra, Karnataka, Gujarat, Delhi, Tamil Nadu
Top 5 FDI Donor Nations to India (April 2000–December 2023)	Mauritius, Singapore, U.S.A, Netherland, Japan

15. Price Indices and Inflation

WPI Index (March 2024) Base 2011–12	151.8
WPI Annual Inflation Rate as on March 2024	0.53%
CPI Industrial workers (Jan 2024) Base 2016	138.9
CPI Agricultural Labourers (Feb 2024) Base 1986–87	1258
CPI Rural Labourers (Feb 2024) Base 1986–87	1269
CPI Rural Index (March 2024) Base 2012	187.7
CPI Urban Index (March 2024) Base 2012	183.6
CPI Combined Index (March 2024) Base 2012	185.8
CPI Inflation Rate (March 2024)	
Rural	5.45
Urban	4.14
Combined	4.85

16. Major Welfare Schemes in India

The Government of India, at all levels, announces Welfare Schemes from time to time for cross sections of the society. These schemes could be either Central, State–specific or a joint collaboration between the Centre and the States. In this section, we are providing quick glance at the several welfare schemes by the Government and their objectives, respectively.

Sr. No.	Scheme	Objective	Launch Date
1	Jawahar Rojgar Yojana (JRY)	■ To generate meaningful employment opportunities to rural youth by creating community assets. ■ Implemented upon the merger of the National Rural Employment Programme (NREP) and Rural Landless Employment Guarantee Programme (RLEGP).	April 1, 1989
2	Employment Assurance Scheme	■ To provide 100 days employment for unskilled manual worker.	October 2, 1993
3	Swaran Jayanti Shahari Rojgar Yojana (SJSRY)	■ To provide gainful employment to the urban unemployed poor through encouraging the setting up of self employment ventures.	December 1, 1997
4	Annapurnan Yojana	■ To provide food security to satisfy the needs of elderly people who are qualified but have not received benefits from the National Old Age Pension Scheme (NOAPS).	March 19, 1999
5	Swaran Jayanti Gram Swarojgar Yojana (SJSRY)	■ To bring the assisted poor families above the poverty line by covering various aspects of self–employment such as organization of the poor into a self–help group, training, credit, technology, infrastructure and marketing. ■ The scheme effectively replaced 6 other schemes: Integrated Rural Development Program (IRDP), Training of Rural Youth for Self–Employment (TRYSEM), Development of Women and Children in Rural Areas (DWCRA), Supply of Improved Toolkits to Rural Artisans (SITRA), Ganga Kalyan Yojana (GKY), and Million Wells Scheme (MWS).	April 1, 1999

(*Contd.*)

Sr. No.	Scheme	Objective	Launch Date
6	Jan Shree Bima Yojana	The scheme aimed at providing **life insurance cover** to rural and urban people below and marginally above the poverty line.	August 10, 2000
7	Antyodaya Anna Yojana	To provide food security to the poorest of poor and end hunger in India.	December 25, 2000
8	Sampoorna Grameen Rozgar Yojana (SGRY)	■ To provide additional and supplementary wage employment, food security and improve nutritional levels in all rural areas. ■ Creation of durable community, social and economic assets in rural areas.	September 25, 2001
9	Pradhan Mantri Gram Sadak Yojana (PMGSY)	To provide connectivity to unconnected Habitations as part of a poverty reduction strategy.	December 25, 2001
10	Social Security Scheme for Labours of Unorganized Sector	The scheme provided three benefits such as, old age pension, medical insurance and accidental insurance to the Labours of Unorganized Sector.	January 23, 2004
11	National food for work program	Launched in 150 most backward districts of India to generate supplementary wage employment.	November 14, 2004
12	Mahatma Gandhi National Rural Employment Guarantee (MGNREGS)	Legal guarantee of a 100 days of wage employment in a financial year to adult members of a rural household who demand employment and are willing to do unskilled manual work.	February 2, 2006
13	Aam Aadmi Bima Yojana	■ Covers natural death/ accidental death, permanent total disability, and partial permanent disability. ■ Provides coverage to individuals residing in rural areas and individuals who are below the poverty line.	August 31, 2007
14	National Rural Livlihood Mission	Promoting self–employment and the organization of rural poor via SHGs.	June 2011
15	National Urban Livlihood Mission	■ Organising urban poor in their strong grassroots level institutions by enhancing sustainable livelihood opportunities through skill development. ■ Replaced the existing Swarna Jayanti Shahari Rozgar Yojana (SJSRY).	September 24, 2013.
16	Pradhan Mantri Jan Dhan Yojana	■ National mission for financial inclusion to ensure access to financial services in an affordable manner. ■ Account can be opened in any bank branch with zero balance.	August 28, 2014
17	Make in India Campaign	■ To create and encourage companies to develop, manufacture and assemble products made in India. ■ To create a conducive environment for investments, develop a modern and efficient infrastructure, and open up new sectors for foreign capital. ■ The initiative targeted 25 economic sectors for job creation and skill enhancement.	September 25, 2014
18	Swachh Bharat Abhiyan	Campaign aimed to achieve the vision of a 'Clean India' by 2nd October 2019.	2 October, 2014
19	Pandit Deendayal Upadhyay Shramev Jayate scheme	To improve the Labor laws and improve the Labor process.	16 October 2014

Sr. No.	Scheme	Objective	Launch Date
20	Pilgrimage Rejuvenation And Spiritual Augmentation Drive (PRASAD)	■ Developing and identifying pilgrimage sites across India for enriching the religious tourism experience. ■ To integrate pilgrimage destinations in a prioritised, planned and sustainable manner to provide a complete religious tourism experience.	2014–15
21	Deendayal Antyodaya Yojana – National Rural Livelihoods Mission (DAY–NRLM)	■ To reduce poverty through building strong institutions for the poor, particularly women, and enabling these institutions to access a range of financial services and livelihoods. Earlier, it was launched in 2011 as Aajeevika – National Rural Livelihoods Mission (NRLM)	2015
22	Sukanaya Samriddhi Yojana	Small deposit scheme by the Ministry of Finance exclusively for a girl child meant to meet the education and marriage expenses of a girl child.	January 22, 2015
23	Beti Bachao Beti Padhao (BBBP)	■ Addresses the declining Child Sex Ratio (CSR) and related issues of women empowerment over a life–cycle continuum. ■ It is a tri–ministerial effort of Ministries of Women and Child Development, Health & Family Welfare and Human Resource Development.	January 22, 2015
24	Pradhan Mantri Kaushal Vikas Yojana (PMKVY)	To encourage and promote skill development in the country by providing free short duration skill training and incentivizing this by providing monetary rewards to youth for skill certification.	16 July, 2015
25	Atal Pension Yojana	The scheme replaces the Swavalamban Yojana and was established to provide old age income security to the workers belonging to the unorganised sector.	9 May, 2015
26	Pradhan Mantri Vaya Vandana Yojana (PMVVY)	■ To provide social security during old age and to protect elderly persons aged 60 and above against a future fall in their interest income due to uncertain market conditions. ■ Provision of assured pension/return linked to the subscription amount based on government guarantee to LI).	July 21, 2017
27	Unnat Bharat Abhiyan	To enable higher educational institutions to work with the people of rural India in identifying development challenges and evolving appropriate solutions for accelerating sustainable growth.	January 12, 2017
28	Pradhan Mantri Kisan Sampada Yojana (PMKSY)	■ To supplement agriculture, modernize processing and decrease Agri–Waste. ■ It is an umbrella scheme incorporating ongoing schemes of the Mega Food Parks, Integrated Cold Chain and Value Addition Infrastructure, Food Safety and Quality Assurance Infrastructure, etc. and also new schemes like Agro–processing Clusters, Creation/Expansion of Food Processing & Preservation Capacities. ■ The scheme was earlier launched with the name of SAMPADA (Scheme for Agro–Marine Processing and Development of Agro–Processing Clusters) in 2017.	May 3, 2017

(Contd.)

Sr. No.	Scheme	Objective	Launch Date
29	Aajeevika Grameen Express Yojana	To offer members of Self Help Groups an alternative household income by facilitating them to operate public transport (e–rickshaws, three and four wheeler motor vehicles) in backward rural areas.	10 August, 2017
30	Saubhagya Yojana	To achieve universal household electrification in the country, through last mile connectivity and providing access to electricity to all un–electrified households in rural areas and poor households in urban areas.	25 September, 2017
31	Rashtriya Krishi Vikas Yojana (RKVY) – Remunerative Approaches for Agriculture and Allied sector Rejuvenation (RAFTAAR)	■ To make farming a remunerative economic activity by strengthening the farmers' efforts, risk mitigation and promoting agri–business entrepreneurship. ■ RKVY scheme was launched in 2007 and was later rebranded as RKVY–RAFTAAR on 1st Nov, 2017.	1 November, 2017
32	Ayushman Bharat Pradhan Mantri Jan Arogya Yojana (PM–JAY)	To provide free access to health insurance coverage for low–income earners in the country.	April 14, 2018
33	GOBAR–Dhan Scheme	Keeping villages clean, increasing the income of rural households and generating energy from cattle waste.	April 30, 2018
34	Regional Connectivity Scheme (RCS) – UDAN (Ude Desh Ka Aam Nagrik)	To improve infrastructure and connectivity in India, especially in remote and underserved regions.	October 21, 2016
35	Bharatmala Pariyojana	An ongoing project that will interconnect 550 District Headquarters and move 80% freight traffic to National Highways by interconnecting 24 logistics parks, 66 inter-corridors, 116 feeder routes and 7 north east Multi–Modal waterway ports.	October 24, 2017
36	Van Dhan Scheme	Launched by Ministry of Tribal Affairs and Tribal Co–Operative Marketing Development Federation of India Limited (TRIFED), it seeks to improve tribal incomes through value addition of tribal products.	14 April, 2018
37	Samagra Shiksha Scheme	To ensure inclusive and equitable quality education from pre–school to senior secondary stage in accordance with the Sustainable Development Goal (SDG) for Education.	May 24, 2018
38	Rashtriya Gram Swaraj Abhiyan	To develop and strengthen the Panchayati Raj System across India in the rural areas	24 April 2018
39	PM KISAN SAMMAN NIDHI (PM–Kisan)	Farmers are given up to ₹6,000 per year as minimum income support.	December 1, 2018
40	Pradhan Mantri Shram Yogi Maandhan (PM–SYM)	Scheme meant for old age protection and social security of Unorganized Workers (UW).	Feb 1, 2019
41	Pradhan Mantri Laghu Vyapari Maan–dhan Yojana	Pension scheme for shopkeeper's/retail traders and self–employed persons for providing monthly minimum assured pension of Rs. 3000/– for the entry age group of 18–40 years	22 July, 2019
42	Pradhan Mantri Kisan Maan Dhan Yojana	To provide an assured monthly pension of Rs. 3000/– to all the small and marginal farmers (who own cultivable land up to 2 hectares) after the age of 60 years.	12 September, 2019

Sr. No.	Scheme	Objective	Launch Date
43	PM–KUSUM (Pradhan Mantri Kisan Urja Suraksha evam Utthaan Mahabhiyan)	Ensuring energy security for farmers in India, along with honouring India's commitment to increase the share of installed capacity of electric power from non–fossil–fuel sources to 40% by 2030 as part of Intended Nationally Determined Contributions (INDCs).	19 February, 2019
44	SUMAN–Surakshit Matritva Aashwasan Yojana	Assured delivery of maternal and newborn healthcare services encompassing wider access to free, and quality services, zero tolerance for denial of services, assured management of complications along with respect for women's autonomy, dignity, feelings, choices and preferences, etc.	10 Oct, 2019
45	NIRVIK (Niryat Rin Vikas Yojana)	To help small scale exporters expand their business.	16 Oct, 2019
46	Atal Bhujal Yojana (Atal Jal)	To improve the management of groundwater resources in select water stressed areas in identified states viz. Gujarat, Haryana, Karnataka, Madhya Pradesh, Maharashtra, Rajasthan and Uttar Pradesh.	12 Dec, 2019
47	Pradhan Mantri Garib Kalyan Yojana	The Pradhan Mantri Garib Kalyan Yojana/Package is a comprehensive relief package of ₹1.70 Lakh Crore Yojana for the poor to help them fight the battle against Corona Virus.	March 26, 2020
48	Atmanirbhar Bharat Abhiyan	■ Making India Self–reliant. ■ It is focused on 5 components – Economy, Infrastructure, Systems, Vibrant Demography and Demand.	13 May, 2020
49	Going Online as Leaders (GOAL) Program	■ Launched by Facebook in partnership with the Ministry of Tribal Affairs (MoTA) on to digitally skill and empower 5000 youth from tribal communities over the next five years. ■ The project aims to identify and mobilise 2500 renowned people from the industry which include policy makers and influencers, teachers, artists, entrepreneurs and social workers known for their achievements in their respective domains, to personally mentor tribal youth across India.	15 May, 2020
50	Garib Kalyan Rojgar Abhiyaan	A massive rural public works scheme of GOI to empower and provide livelihood opportunities to the returnee migrant workers and rural citizens.	20 June, 2020
51	Sahkar Mitra Scheme	A scheme by National Cooperative Development Corporation (NCDC) on Internship Program" (SIP) is an arrangement where NCDC will provide short term (not exceeding four months) opportunities to young professionals to acquire learning experience by applying skills and knowledge in an organisational context to facilitate professional development.	June 12, 2020

(Contd.)

Sr. No.	Scheme	Objective	Launch Date
52	PM Street Vendor's AtmaNirbhar Nidhi (PM SVANidhi)	■ Launched by the Ministry of Housing and Urban Affairs for providing affordable Working Capital loan to street vendors to resume their livelihoods that were adversely affected due to COVID–19 lockdown. ■ The scheme intends to facilitate collateral free working capital loans of up to INR10,000/– of one–year tenure, to approximately 50 lakh street vendors, to help resume their businesses in the urban areas, including surrounding peri–urban/rural areas.	June 1, 2020
53	PM Atmanirbhar Swasth Bharat Scheme	■ To develop capacities of primary, secondary, and tertiary care health systems even in the last miles of the nation. ■ Developing a modern ecosystem for research, testing and treatment in the country itself.	Feb 1, 2021
54	e–RUPI digital payment solution	■ National Payments Corporation of India (NPCI) in association with Department of Financial Services (DFS), National Health Authority (NHA), Ministry of Health and Family Welfare (MoHFW), and partner banks, has launched an innovative digital solution – 'e–RUPI'. ■ The users of this seamless one–time payment mechanism will be able to redeem the voucher without a card, digital payments app or internet banking access, at the merchants accepting e–RUPI.	August 2, 2021
55	MeitY SAMRIDH Scheme	■ To provide funding support to Startups so that they can become successful. ■ Acceleration will be provided to startups by providing skillsets, customer connect, investor connects and international connect services.	August 25, 2021
56	PM CARES for Children Scheme	■ To support children who have lost both the Parents or legal Guardian or Adoptive Parents or Surviving Parent to COVID–19 pandemic during the period starting from 11th March 2020 to 28th February, 2022. ■ To ensure comprehensive care and protection of children in a sustained manner, and enable their well–being through health insurance, empower them through education and equip them for self–sufficient existence with financial support on reaching 23 years of age.	29 May, 2021
57	Surakshit Hum Surakshit Tum Abhiyaan	NITI Aayog and Piramal Foundation launched Surakshit Hum Surakshit Tum Abhiyaan in 112 Aspirational Districts to assist district administrations in providing home–care support to COVID–19 patients who are asymptomatic or have mild symptoms.	June 8, 2021

Sr. No.	Scheme	Objective	Launch Date
58	National Mission for Edible Oils – Oil Palm (NMEO–OP)	■ To promote oil palm in new geographies, providing end–to–end support to farmers in terms of assistance in planting material, assured buyback from private players involved, and protecting the farmers from the global price volatility in oil palm by providing viability gap payment (VGP) to hedge farmers' risk. ■ To escalate oil palm cultivation and elevating Crude Palm Oil production to 11.20 lakh tonnes by 2025–26.	August 18, 2021
59	Mission Poshan 2.0	■ An umbrella scheme covering the Integrated Child Development Services (ICDS) (Anganwadi Services, Poshan Abhiyan, Scheme For Adolescent Girls, National Creche Scheme). ■ Launched to strengthen nutritional content, delivery, outreach and outcome, with renewed focus on developing practices that nurture health, wellness and immunity to disease and malnutrition in the country.	March 8, 2021
60	Jal Jeevan Mission	■ Goal of achieving Har Ghar Jal by 2024. ■ It envisages supply of 55 litres of water per person per day to every rural household through Functional Household Tap Connections (FHTC) by 2024.	Feb 1, 2021
61	SVAMITVA (Survey of Villages and Mapping with Improvised Technology in Village Areas) Scheme	■ It is a scheme for mapping the land parcels in rural inhabited areas using drone technology and Continuously Operating Reference Station (CORS). ■ The mapping will be done across the country in a phase–wise manner over a period of four years – from 2020 to 2024.	April 24, 2021
62	Production Linked Incentive Scheme (PLI)	■ To scale up domestic manufacturing capability, accompanied by higher import substitution and employment generation. ■ Covers about14 sectors. ■ Domestic and Foreign companies receive financial rewards for manufacturing in India, based on a percentage of their revenue over up to five years.	October 16, 2021
63	National Rail Plan (NRP) for India – 2030	■ To create a 'future ready' Railway system by 2030. ■ To create capacity ahead of demand, which in turn would also cater to future growth in demand right up to 2050 and also increase the modal share of Railways to 45% in freight traffic and to continue to sustain it.	
64	National Green Hydrogen Mission	To accelerate the deployment of Green Hydrogen as a clean energy source, will support the development of supply chains that can efficiently transport and distribute hydrogen.	Feb 1, 2021
65	One Nation One Ration Card (ONORC) Scheme	■ The scheme allows all NFSA beneficiaries, particularly migrant beneficiaries, to claim either full or part foodgrains from any Fair Price Shop (FPS) in the country through existing ration card with biometric/ Aadhaar authentication in a seamless manner. ■ The system also allows their family members back home, if any, to claim the balance foodgrains on same the ration card.	August, 2019

(*Contd.*)

Sr. No.	Scheme	Objective	Launch Date
66	Ayushman Bharat Digital Mission	It aims to provide digital health IDs for all Indian citizens to help hospitals, insurance firms, and citizens access health records electronically when required.	Sept 27, 2021
67	Atal Mission for Rejuvenation and Urban Transformation (AMRUT) 2.0 Scheme	■ Continuation of the AMRUT mission launched in June 2015, AMRUT 2.0 aims to provide 100% coverage of water supply to all households in around 4,700/Urban Local Bodies. ■ It also seeks to promote Atmanirbhar Bharat through encouraging Startups and Entrepreneurs (Public Private Partnership).	October 1, 2021
68	Support for Marginalized Individuals for Livelihood and Enterprise (SMILE)	Central Sector Scheme for Comprehensive Rehabilitation for the Welfare of Transgender Persons.	Feb 12, 2022
69	Scheme for Economic Empowerment of Denotified, Nomadic and Semi–Nomadic Tribes (SEED)	To provide free competitive exam coaching to these students, to provide health insurance to families, to uplift clusters of these communities through livelihood initiatives, and to provide financial assistance for housing.	Feb 16, 2022
70	Scheme for Residential Education for Students in High Schools in Targeted Areas (SHRESHTA)	To fill the educational service gap in Scheduled Castes (SCs) dominant areas by providing high–quality education, socio–economic upliftment, and overall development for SC students.	June 3, 2022
71	Pradhan Mantri Bhartiya Jana Urvarak Pariyojana (PM–BJUR)	Objectives of the scheme are: ■ One Nation One Fertiliser (ONOF). ■ To **initiate more than 3.25 lakh fertiliser shops** across the country as Pradhan Mantri Sammridhi Kendra. These centres will provide ancillary services like **soil testing, information about soil testing**, etc. ■ With this scheme, all the confusion regarding the standards and quality of the product would come to an end. Now all the urea across the country will bear the same name, quality and logo. ■ The jurisdiction of this project covers both the private and the public sector companies in India.	October 17, 2022
72	Jadui Pitara	■ A play–based learning–teaching material tailored for children between the age group of 3–8 years. ■ It comprises playbooks, toys, puzzles, posters, flash cards, story books etc., and has been developed under the National Curriculum Framework (NCF) and is available in 13 Indian languages.	Feb 20, 2023
73	PM Vishwakarma Scheme	■ To provide end–to–end support to artisans and craftspeople who work with their hands and tools. ■ The Scheme covers artisans and craftspeople engaged in 18 trades.	Sept 17, 2023
74	PM e–bus seva	To augment bus operations by deployment of 10,000 electric buses on PPP model.	August 16, 2023

UNIT II
ECONOMIC SURVEY & BUDGET

The budget should be balanced not by more taxes, but by reduction of follies.
—Herbert Hoover

Economic Survey and Budget are considered noteworthy financial and economic documents of the country. The Economic Survey is the flagship document of the Ministry of Finance and tabled in the Parliament a day before the Union Budget every year. It gives a detailed account of various sectors of the economy and overall economic scenario of the country in the past years and provides an outline for the year ahead. It summarizes the performance on major development programs, highlights the policy initiatives of the government, and analyzes the prospects of the economy in the short to medium term. Increasingly, it has also become a forum for analysis and research on the economy, and hence, also a source of policy ideas.

On the other hand, the budget is described as a precise statement, representing a financial estimate of income and expenditure of the government for the coming year.* Depending on the feasibility of these estimates, budgets are of three types—balanced budget, surplus budget, and deficit budget. A government budget is said to be a balanced budget if the estimated government expenditure is equal to the expected government receipts in a particular financial year. Classical economists were advocates of balanced budget. A government budget is said to be a surplus budget if the expected government revenues exceed the estimated government expenditure in a particular financial year. A surplus budget denotes the financial affluence of a country. Such a budget can be implemented at times of inflation to reduce aggregate demand. A government budget is said to be a deficit budget if the estimated government expenditure exceeds the expected government revenue in a particular financial year. Modern day governments are welfare governments, and therefore, their budgets are deficit budgets.

BUDGET 2024–25

Q1. What is the focus of Budget 2024–25?
Ans. The four major castes where Budget lays its focus are Garib (Poor), Mahilayen (Women), Yuva (Youth), Annadata (Farmer)

Q2. What are the priorities of Budget 2024–25?
Ans. Budget 2024–25 has nine priorities. They are—Productivity and resilience in Agriculture; Employment & Skilling; Inclusive Human Resource Development and Social Justice; Manufacturing & Services; Urban Development; Energy Security; Infrastructure; Innovation, Research & Development; and Next Generation Reforms.

Q3. What is the total size of Budget 2024–25?
Ans. The total size of budget 2024–25 is ₹48.21 Lakh Crore.

Following is the display of Budget in the form of receipts and expenditure.

Receipts and Expenditure (in crore)

1. **Revenue Receipts**	3129200
2. Tax Revenue (Net to Centre)	2583499
3. Non-Tax Revenue	545701
4. **Capital Receipts**	1691312
5. Recovery of Loans	28000
6. Other Receipts	50000

* For the detailed discussion of Budget and its components please refer to chapter 25 Public Expenditure, Debt Management and Fiscal Policy in the main book.

7. Borrowings and Other Liabilities	1613312
8. **Total Receipts (1+4)**	4820512
9. **Total Expenditure (10+13)**	4820512
10. On Revenue Account of which	3709401
11. Interest Payments	1162940
12. Grants in aid for creation of Capital Account	390778
13. On Capital Account	1111111

Q4. Where are the sources of budget receipts in 2024–25?
Ans. Following are the sources of rupee generation of budget 2024–25.

Rupee Comes From

Borrowing and other liabilities	27%
Income Tax	19%
GST and other Taxes	18%
Corporation Taxes	17%
Non-tax receipts	9%
Union Excise Duty	5%
Customs	4%
Non-debt capital receipts	1%

Q5. Where are the proposed spendings as per budget 2024–25?
Ans. Following are the proposed spendings as per budget 20204–25.

Rupee Goes To

States' share of taxes and duties	21%
Interest Payments	19%
Central Sector Scheme	16%
Other Expenditure	9%
Finance commission & other transfers	9%
Centrally sponsored schemes	8%
Defense	8%
Subsidy	6%
Pensions	4%

Q6. What are the deficit trends as per budget 2024–25?
Ans. Following are the deficit trends as per budget for the year 2024–25.

Deficit Trends

Deficits	**₹ (crore)**	**As a % of GDP**
Fiscal Deficit	1613313	4.9%
Revenue Deficit	580201	1.8%
Effective Revenue Deficit	189423	0.6%
Primary Deficit	450372	1.4%

Q7. What are the direct tax proposals in the budget 2024–25?

Ans. Following are the direct tax proposals in the budget 2024–25:

- The Budget 2024 has revised the tax slabs in the New Regime, providing taxpayers with an extra opportunity to save ₹17,500 in taxes.
- The standard deduction has been raised to ₹75,000.
- The family pension deduction has been increased to ₹25,000 from ₹15,000.
- Short term gains of financial assets to attract 20% tax rate.
- Long term gains on all financial a non-financial assets to attract a tax rate of 12.5%
- Increase in limit of exemption of capital gains on financial assets to ₹1.25 lakh per year.
- ANGEL tax for all classes of investors abolished.
- Corporate tax rate on foreign companies reduced from 40% to 35%.

Q8. What is the new tax slab as per budget 2024–25? How is it different from previous regime?

Ans. The new tax regime is different from previous year tax regime as following:

FY 2023–24		FY 2024–25	
Tax Slab	**Tax Rate**	**Tax Slab**	**Tax Rate**
Upto ₹3 lakh	Nil	Upto ₹3 lakh	Nil
₹3 lakh – ₹6 lakh	5%	₹3 lakh – ₹7 lakh	5%
₹6 lakh – ₹9 lakh	10%	₹7 lakh – ₹10 lakh	10%
₹9 lakh – ₹12 lakh	15%	₹10 lakh – ₹12 lakh	15%
₹12 lakh – ₹15 lakh	20%	₹12 lakh – ₹15 lakh	20%
More than 15 lakh	30%	More than 15 lakh	30%

Q9. What are Indirect Tax Proposals?

Ans. Following is the detail with regard to Indirect taxes as per budget 2024–25.

- 3 more cancer medicines from custom duties exempted.
- Basic custom duty (BCD) reduced to 15% on Mobile phone, Mobile PCBA and charger.
- BCD reduced on gold and silver to 6% and platinum to 6.4%.
- BCD reduced on shrimp and fish feed to 5%.
- More capital goods for manufacturing of solar cells & panels exempted.
- Custom duties on 25 critical minerals fully exempted.

Q11. What steps have been taken to promote productivity of Agriculture?

Ans. Following steps have been taken to promote productivity of Indian Agriculture in the budget 2024–25.

- A provision of ₹1.52 lakh crore for agriculture and allied sector.
- Comprehensive review of the agriculture research setup to bring focus on raising productivity and developing climate resilient varieties.
- New 109 high-yielding and climate-resilient varieties of 32 field and horticulture crops will be released for cultivation by farmers.
- In the next two years, 1 crore farmers across the country will be initiated into natural farming supported by certification and branding with the help of scientific institutions and willing gram panchayats. 10,000 need-based bio-input resource centres will be established.
- Strategy to achieve *'atmanirbharta'* for oil seeds such as mustard, groundnut, sesame, soybean, and sunflower.
- Promotion of FPOs, cooperatives & start-ups for vegetable supply chains for collection, storage, and marketing.

- Digital Public Infrastructure (DPI) for coverage of farmers and their lands in 3 years. Digital crop survey will be conducted in 400 districts and issuance of *Jan Samarth* based Kisan Credit Cards.
- To promote shrimp farming and export, finance will be facilitated through NABARD.
- National Cooperation Policy will be announced for systematic, orderly and all-round development of the cooperative sector.

Q12. What is proposed in the budget to promote employment and skilling?
Ans. Under employment and skilling the budget 2024–25 has formulated three-pronged strategy which is as under.

I. Employment Linked Incentive
There will be three schemes under Employment linked incentives.

Scheme A: First Timers: One-month wage to new entrants in all formal sectors in 3 instalments up to ₹15,000; expected to benefit 210 lakh youth.

Scheme B: Job Creation in Manufacturing: Linked to first time employees; Incentive to both employee & employer for EPFO contributions in the specified scales for the first 4 years; Expected to benefit 30 lakh youth.

Scheme C: Support to Employers: Government will reimburse EPFO contributions of employers up to ₹3000 per month for 2 years for all new hires; Expected to generate 50 lakh jobs.

II. Skilling Programme

- 20 lakh youth will be skilled over a 5-year period.
- 1,000 Industrial Training Institutes will be upgraded in hub and spoke arrangements with outcome orientation.
- Course content & design aligned as per skill needs of industry.

III. Other Programs:

- **Women** in the workforce through setting up of working women hostels in collaboration with industry, and establishing creches.
- Loans up to ₹7.5 lakh with a guarantee from a government promoted Fund. Expected to help 25,000 students every year.
- Financial support for loans upto ₹10 lakh for higher education in domestic institutions.
- Direct E-vouchers to 1 lakh students every year. Annual interest subvention of 3%

Q13. What is Purvodaya plan as announced in the budget 2024–25?
Purvodaya plan includes following developmental activities:

- It is plan for the all-round development of the eastern region of the country covering states like Bihar, Jharkhand, West Bengal, Odisha and Andhra Pradesh for generation of economic opportunities to attain Viksit Bharat.
- An industrial node at Gaya will be developed at Amritsar Kolkata Industrial Corridor.
- Development of road connectivity projects will be supported, namely (1) Patna-Purnea Expressway, (2) Buxar-Bhagalpur Expressway, (3) Bodhgaya, Rajgir, Vaishali and Darbhanga spurs, and (4) additional 2-lane bridge over river Ganga at Buxar at a total cost of ₹26,000 crore.
- Power projects, including setting up of a new 2400 MW power plant at Pirpainti, will be taken up at a cost of ₹21,400 crore.
- New airports, medical colleges and sports infrastructure in Bihar will be constructed.
- The requests of Bihar Government for external assistance from multilateral development banks will be expedited.

Q14. What has budget 2024–25 proposed to fulfil the commitments in the Andhra Pradesh Reorganization Act?

Ans. The budget 2024–25 lays down following commitments:

- Financial support of ₹15,000 crores will be arranged in FY 24–25.
- Completion of Polavaram Irrigation Project ensuring food security of the nation.
- Essential infrastructure such as water, power, railways and roads in Kopparthy node on the Vishakhapatnam-Chennai Industrial Corridor and Orvakal node on Hyderabad-Bengaluru Industrial Corridor.
- Grants for backward regions of Rayalaseema, Prakasam and North Coastal Andhra will be provided.

Q15. What has government proposed for manufacturing and Services?

The proposals for manufacturing and Services can be discussed under three heads:

I. Schemes for MSMEs:

- Credit Guarantee Scheme for MSMEs in the Manufacturing Sector.
- Enhanced scope for mandatory onboarding in TReDS.
- MSME Units for Food Irradiation, Quality & Safety Testing.
- New assessment model for MSME credit.
- Mudra Loans: The limit enhanced to ₹20 lakh from the current ₹10 lakh under the 'Tarun' category.
- Credit Support to MSMEs during Stress Period.

II. Internship Opportunities

- Scheme for providing internship opportunities in 500 top companies to 1 crore youth in 5 years.
- Allowance of ₹5,000 per month along with a one-time assistance of ₹6,000 through the CSR funds.

III. Other Schemes

- Twelve industrial parks under the National Industrial Corridor Development Programme.
- Rental housing with dormitory type accommodation for industrial workers in PPP mode with VGF support.
- Critical Minerals Mission for domestic production, recycling and overseas acquisition.
- Strengthening of the tribunal and appellate tribunals to speed up insolvency resolution and additional tribunals to be established

Q16. What steps have been proposed for urban development?

Ans. Urban development proposals can be discussed under five heads:

- **Stamp Duty:** Encouraging states to lower stamp duties for properties purchased by women.
- **Street Markets:** Envisioning a scheme to develop 100 weekly 'haats' or street food hubs in select cities.
- **Transit Oriented Development:** Transit Oriented Development plans for 14 large cities with a population above 30 lakh.
- **Water Management:** Promote water supply, sewage treatment and solid waste management projects and services for 100 large cities through bankable projects.
- **Housing Needs:** Under the PM Awas Yojana Urban 2.0, housing needs of 1 crore urban poor and middle-class families will be addressed with an investment of ₹10 lakh crore. Enabling policies and regulations for efficient and **transparent rental housing markets** with enhanced availability will also be put in place.

Q17. What proposals have been made to promote Energy Security in the country?
Ans. Following proposals have been made to promote Energy Security.

- **Nuclear Energy:** Setting up Bharat Small Reactors; R&D of Bharat Small Modular Reactor and newer technologies for nuclear energy.
- **Energy Audit:** Financial support for shifting of micro and small industries to cleaner forms of energy; Facilitate investment grade energy audit in 60 clusters, next phase expands to 100 clusters.
- **Pumped Storage Policy:** For electricity storage and facilitation of smooth integration of the growing share of renewable energy.
- **AUSC Thermal Power Plants:** A joint venture between NTPC and BHEL will set up a full scale 800 MW commercial plant.
- **PM Surya Ghar Muft Bijli Yojana:** The scheme is already launched to install rooftop solar plants to enable 1 crore households obtain free electricity up to 300 units every month.

Q18. What are the proposals for Infrastructure development?
Ans. The proposals for Infrastructure Investment can be discussed under four heads:

I. Infrastructure Investment

- Provision of **₹11,11,111** crore for infrastructure (3.4% of GDP).
- **₹1.5** lakh crore to states as long term interest free loans to support resource allocation.

II. Pradhan Mantri Gram Sadak Yojana (PMGSY)

- **Phase IV** of PMGSY will be launched to provide all weather connectivity to **25,000** rural habitations.

III. Irrigation and Flood Mitigation

- Financial support for projects with estimated cost of ₹11,500 crore such as the **Kosi-Mechi** intra-state link and 20 other ongoing and new schemes.
- Assistance for flood management and related projects in Assam, Sikkim & Uttarakhand.
- Assistance for reconstruction and rehabilitation in Himachal Pradesh.

IV. Tourism

- Development of Vishnupad Temple Corridor and Mahabodhi Temple Corridor modelled on Kashi Vishwanath Temple Corridor.
- Comprehensive development initiative for Rajgir will be undertaken which holds religious significance for Hindus, Buddhists and Jains.
- The development of Nalanda as a tourist centre besides reviving Nalanda University to its glorious stature.
- Assistance to development of Odisha's scenic beauty, temples, monuments, craftsmanship, wildlife sanctuaries, natural landscapes and pristine beaches making it an ultimate tourism destination.

Q19. What steps have been taken in the budget to promote Innovation, Research & Development?
Ans. Following steps have been taken to promote Innovation, Research & Development.

- Private sector-driven research and innovation at commercial scale with a financing pool of ₹1 lakh crore.
- A venture capital fund of ₹1,000 crore is to be set up to promote space economy.

Q20. What are the Next Generation Reforms as proposed in the budget?
Ans. The next generation reforms can be discussed in six heads:

I. Rural & Urban land related actions
Unique Land Parcel Identification Number or Bhu-Aadhaar for all lands; Survey of map sub-divisions as per current ownership; Linkages to the farmers' registries; Land records in urban areas will be digitized with GIS mapping; Digitization of cadastral maps; Establishment of land registry.

II. Taxonomy for climate finance
Enhancing the availability of capital for climate adaptation and mitigation related investments.

III. FDI and Overseas Investments: Simplified to facilitate FDIs and promote opportunities for using Indian Rupee as a currency for overseas investments.

IV. NPS Vatsalya: A plan for contribution by parents and guardians for minors.

V. Data related reforms: Improvement of data governance, collection, processing and management of data and statistics.

VI. New Pension Scheme (NPS): A solution that address the relevant issues, protects the common citizen and maintains fiscal prudence will be formed.

ECONOMIC SURVEY 2023–24

Q1. What are the trends in Global Macroeconomic Indicators?
Ans. The trends in Global Macroeconomic Indicators:

- The global economy registered a growth of 3.2 per cent in 2023, whereas the global GDP growth for advanced economies and emerging market and developing economies is 1.6 and 4.3% respectively.
- All major economies have surpassed pre-pandemic GDP levels.
- The Red Sea crisis amid heightened geopolitical tensions in the Middle East eased a year later leading to decline in inflationary pressure.
- Headline inflation across countries declined, however, core inflation remained sticky on account of services inflation and a strong labour market, especially in most advanced economies. The persistence of core inflation prompted many central banks to maintain policy rates at a high level or further increase them in 2023.
- Global general government fiscal deficit (as a per cent of GDP) rose by 1.6 percentage points in 2023 compared to 2022.
- The global volume of exports of goods and services registered a modest growth of 0.5 per cent in 2023 compared to 2022.
- Global FDI flows declined in 2023 as compared to 2022 due to high geopolitical conflicts, high borrowing costs and global economic fracturing.

Q2. Why India's GDP growth has shown resilience and is expected to remain robust?
Ans. During the post covid years, India Economy has grown at the rate of 9.7, 7.0, 8.2 per cent respectively for the financial years 2021–22, 2022–23 and 2023–24. For the FY 2024–25, the economy is expected to grow between 6.5 to 7.0% respectively. According to economic survey, steady private consumption and emerging investment are the major drivers of growth. Following factors can be attributed to resilience and robust growth of the economy.

- The share of private consumption in total GDP of the country at current prices is 60.3% and that of investment is 30.8%. Exports contribute 29.1% to total GDP growth.
- Investment being driven by public and private capex with households also pitching in. For example, Household savings in physical assets as % of GDP up from 10.8% in FY21 to 12.9% in FY23.

- Quality of Union Government expenditure is improving. For example, capital expenditure has grown from 12 to 21% during FY 2021 to 2025. Moreover, decomposition of fiscal deficit shows increasing investment orientation as capital outlay as a % of total fiscal deficit has increased from 43 to 47.6% during FY 2019 to 2025.
- Relatively low domestic inflation, high growth and stable external sector are imparting resilience to the economy.

Q3. Discuss the trends in Union Govt's receipts and expenditure?
Ans.

A. <u>Trends in Receipts</u>

I. Consolidation of Union Government Finances

- Fiscal, revenue and primary deficits have declined to 5.6, 2.6 and 2.0 per cent respectively in 2023 as compared to 2022.
- A decomposition of the fiscal deficit over the past few years reveals that with a narrowing revenue deficit, nearly 48 per cent of the fiscal deficit is being accounted for by capital outlay. This suggests that the productivity of borrowed resources has improved.

II. Buoyancy in revenues continues in FY24

- Revenue receipts of the union government increased YoY by 14.5 per cent in FY24, with robust growth in both tax and non-tax revenues.
- Increase in gross tax revenue to GDP (11.7%) is driven by strong direct tax growth.
- There is increase in indirect taxes in FY24 mainly driven by a 12.7 per cent growth in GST collection.

B. <u>Trends in Expenditure</u>

- Total expenditure declined to 15.0 per cent of GDP in FY24 from 17.7 per cent in FY21.
- The capital expenditure for FY24 stood at ₹9.5 lakh crore, an increase of 28.2 per cent on a YoY basis, and was 2.8 times the level of FY20.
- Expenditure on major subsidies declined by 22.1 per cent on a YoY basis, led by a decrease in fertiliser and food subsidies respectively, in FY24.

Q4. Discuss the trends in Money Supply during 2023–24.
Ans. The trends in Money Supply are as following:

- There is increase of Reserve Money (M0) due to increase in net foreign assets.
- The growth in Broad Money (M3) was 11.2 per cent during March 2024, compared to 9 per cent a year ago. Amongst sources, bank credit to the commercial sector significantly contributed to the increase in M3, with a share of 67.1 per cent, supplemented by net bank credit to the Government (29.4 per cent).
- The Monetary Policy Committee (MPC) maintained the status quo on the policy repo rate at 6.5 per cent in FY24.
- Nearly 98 per cent of the ₹2,000 denomination banknotes have returned to the banking system causing acceleration in aggregate deposits and broad money (M3).
- As of 22 March 2024, the Money Multiplier (MM) was 5.4 against 5.2 a year ago.

Q5. How Microfinance development in India led to financial inclusion in the country?
Ans. Microfinance development in India has led to financial inclusion in the following way.

- There is rise in loans disbursed by MFIs from 0.8 to 1.8 Lakh crore from FY13 to FY23.
- India has the second-largest microfinance sector.

- Women constitute 98 per cent of the total clients of MFIs.
- MFIs have reached out to over 532 lakh clients with a total loan outstanding of ₹1.8 lakh crore under micro-credit.
- Rise in RBI's Financial Inclusion Index from 60.1 in March 2023 to 64.2 in March 2024 indicates improvement in access, usage, and quality of the financial sector in India.

Q6. In what ways Indian capital market emerged as one of the best-performing among emerging markets in FY24?

Ans. Following are the salient features of capital market:

- **Primary Markets:** Primary markets facilitated capital formation of ₹10.9 lakh crore in FY24, compared to ₹9.3 lakh crore in FY23.
- **Secondary Markets:** India's Nifty 50 index ascended by 26.8 per cent during FY24, as against (–)8.2 % during FY23.
- **Market Capitalisation:** India's market capitalisation to GDP ratio improved significantly from 77 % in FY19 to 124 % in FY24.
- **Mutual Funds:** Assets under Management of mutual funds increased by ₹14 lakh crore to ₹53.4 lakh crore at the end of FY24.
- **Systematic Investment Plan:** Annual net SIP flows more than doubled from ₹0.96 lakh crore in FY21 to ₹2 lakh crore in FY24.

Q7. What are the trends of Inflation in India? Discuss the steps taken to control Inflation.

Ans. India's retail headline, core and food inflation for the year 2023 is reported to be 5.4, 4.3 and 7.5 per cent respectively. It was lower than emerging market and developing economies (EMDEs). Following steps have been taken at different levels to contain inflation.

- Repo rate has been increased from 4 to 6.5% during 2020 to 2023.
- Lowered LPG and fuel prices.
- Export Prohibition on cereals, onion and sugar.
- Stock monitoring of cereals and pulses.
- Subsidised sale of cereals, pulses and onion.
- Reduction of import duty on pulses and edible oil.

Q8. Discuss the trends of food inflation in India.

Ans. Food inflation based on the Consumer Food Price Index (CFPI) increased from 3.8 per cent in FY22 to 6.6 per cent in FY23 and further to 7.5 per cent in FY24. Following are the causes of rising food prices. The production prospects of vegetables and pulses were particularly impacted by unfavourable weather conditions. Increase in the price of milk took place due to a decrease in artificial inseminations during the peak days of the pandemic, and higher costs for animal feed. As 50 per cent of the total edible oil requirement is being imported, the global inflation affects its prices.

Q9. What are the achievements of service sector of India?

Ans. Following are the achievements of service sector:

- India's services exports more than doubled in nine years. The service sector exports have increased from 158 to 341 billion USD during FY15 to FY24.
- India's services exports share in world services exports is 4.3%. India had second rank in World's telecommunication, computer & information services exports.
- India has 6th rank in World's personal, cultural & recreational services exports. India has 8th rank in world's other business service exports.
- India's rank in World Bank's logistics performance has improved from 44th in 2018 to 38th in 2023.

Q10. How can India benefit from China plus one strategy?

Ans. China plus one strategy refers to the global trend where companies diversify their manufacturing and supply chains by establishing operations in countries other than China. India can benefit from China plus one strategy by promoting FDI from China and by reducing imports dependence from China. There is evidence of trade diversion from China as reflected in an increase in India's electronic exports to US, resulting in a rise in trade surplus.

Q11. Discuss the trends of India's foreign trade.

- India's share in global goods exports was 1.8 per cent in FY24, against an average of 1.7 per cent during FY16–FY20. Similarly, its share in global services exports rose to 4.3 per cent in FY23 from an average of 3.3 per cent during FY16–FY20.
- Merchandise exports rose to USD 437 billion in FY24, whereas merchandise imports contracted from USD 716 billion in FY23 to USD 675.4 billion in FY24.
- In FY24, UAE, Singapore, China, Russia, and Australia emerged as India's major export partners.

Q12. What are the indicators of India's Stable External Sector?

Ans. Following are the indicators of India's Stable External Sector.

- Decline in External debt to GDP ratio from nearly 24% in 2015 to 19% of GDP in 2024.
- India witnessed the most significant increase in foreign exchange reserves holdings of 68 billion USD during April 23 to March 2024.
- Highest level of FPI inflows witnessed in FY24 (44.1 billion USD) after FY15 (42.2 billion USD).
- Current account surplus in Q4 of FY24 led to a moderation in current account deficit in FY24.
- India emerged as the top remittance recipient in the World in 2023.
- Robust foreign inflows and comfortable trade deficits are expected to keep the rupee stable as well as within a comfortable range.

Q13. What are the latest trends in Indian Agriculture Sector?

Ans. The latest trends in India's Agriculture Sector are as under:

- Agriculture and allied sector registered an average annual growth rate of 4.18 per cent at constant prices over the last five years.
- The growth rate of the agriculture sector stood at 1.4 per cent in 2023–24, which is below 4.7 per cent in 2022–23.
- Foodgrain production was reported to be 329.7 million tonnes in 2022–23, and 328.8 million tonnes in 2023–24.
- Oilseeds production was reported to be reached 41.4 million tonnes in 2023–24.
- The allied sectors of Indian agriculture are steadily emerging as robust growth centres and promising sources for improving farm incomes.
- As of 31 January 2024, the total credit disbursed to agriculture amounted to ₹22.84 lakh Crore.
- As of January 31, 2024, banks issued 7.5 crores Kisan Credit Card (KCC) with a limit of ₹9.4 lakh crores.
- An area of 90.0 lakh hectares has been covered under micro irrigation in the country under the Per drop more crop (PDMC) from 2015–16 to 2023–24.
- It is estimated that for every rupee invested in agricultural research (including education), there is a payoff of ₹13.85.

Q14. What are the reasons of resilient Agriculture Sector Growth?

Ans. The Indian agriculture sector provides livelihood support to about 42.3 per cent of the population and has a share of 18.2 per cent in the country's GDP at current prices. The sector has been buoyant, which is evident from the fact that it has registered an average annual growth rate of 4.18 per cent at constant prices over the last five years. Reasons for buoyant growth are:

- Fixing MSP at one and half times the all-India weighted average cost of production-assuring remunerative prices to farmers.
- The allied sectors of Indian agriculture are steadily emerging as robust growth centres and promising sources for improving farm incomes.
- Growth in the livestock sector significantly boosted the per capita availability of milk, eggs, and meat.
- The fisheries sector has grown at a compound annual rate of 8.9 per cent between 2014–15 and 2022–23 (at constant prices).

Q15. What is farmer-friendly policy framework as suggested by Economic Survey?

Ans. Survey provides five policy recommendations that the markets function in the interest of the farmer.

- Not banning futures or options at the first sign of price spikes.
- Invoking export bans only under exceptional circumstances and allowing domestic consumers to substitute, especially if the agricultural commodities in question are not essential consumption items such as foodgrains.
- India's inflation targeting framework should consider targeting inflation, excluding food as higher food prices are, more often, not demand-induced but supply-induced. Hardships caused by higher food prices for poor can be handled through welfare policies.
- Need for increasing the Total Net Irrigated Area as several states are well below the national average and India's irrigation efficiency is only 30–40 per cent for surface water and 50–60 per cent for groundwater,
- Making farming consistent with climate considerations. Grains such as rice and sugarcane are water-guzzling crops and cultivation of paddy gives rise to methane emissions.

Q16. What are the trends in food-processing sector?

- The GVA of the food processing sector was ₹1.92 lakh crore in 2022–23 and it constituted 7.66 per cent of GVA in Manufacturing in 2022–23.
- India is the largest producer of milk and the second largest producer of fruits, vegetables and sugar.
- The food processing industry in India is one of the largest employers in organized manufacturing, with a 12.02 per cent share in the total employment in the organised sector.
- The value of agri-food exports, including processed food exports during 2022–23, was USD46.44Billion, accounting for about 11.7 per cent of India's total exports.
- The share of processed food exports also increased from 14.9 per cent in 2017–18 to 23.4 per cent in 2022–23.

Q17. What is the Growth Strategy for Amrit Kaala as envisaged in Economic Survey 2023–24?

Ans. The growth strategy is as under:

- Boost private sector investment to 35 per cent of GDP through a 1 conducive policy and regulatory environment.
- Strengthen India's MSME sector through deregulation at the state and local government levels. Push for sector-specific, tailored skilling of MSME entrepreneurs and developing a clear-cut export strategy.
- Remove growth impediments in the agricultural sector and allow markets 3 to function in the interest of the farmer.
- Secure financing of green transition in India.
- Bridge the education – employment gap.
- Build state capacity and capability.

Q18. Write a note on PM-Surya Ghar Yojana?

Ans. The Prime Minister had launched the scheme on 13th February, 2024. The scheme has the following characteristics. Total outlay of ₹75,021 crore; Installing rooftop solar; Free electricity up to 300 units every month for 1 crore households; Create around 17 lakh direct jobs; Addition of 30 GW of solar capacity through rooftop solar; and Reduction of 720 million tonnes of CO2 equivalent emissions.

Q19. What is the state of mental health in India?

- Globally, one out of every two people will develop a mental health disorder in their lifetime. 10.6 per cent adults suffered from mental disorders in India, Treatment gap of 70–92%.
- Youth and phone/Internet overuse and 'great rewiring of childhood'.
- Economic Impact: productivity loss, healthcare cost, higher risk with rising urbanisation and demographic dividend.
- Policy action: National Mental Health Programme and Ayushman Bharat.
- Need for adequate personnel, breaking the stigma, community action.

Q20. Why is India called Pharmacy of the world?

Ans. India is called pharmacy of the world because of the following:

- India's pharmaceutical market currently valued at USD 50 Billion is the world's third largest by volume.
- There are around 60,000 generic brands across 60 therapeutic categories, accounting for 20 per cent of global generic drug exports by volume.
- Eight of the top 20 global generic companies are based in India.
- India's pharmaceutical sector boasts high rates of quality compliance, with 703 US FDA approved facilities (as of April 2023), 38612 European GMP-compliant plants (as of November 2022) and 241813 WHO-GMP-approved plants.
- During FY24, the value of export and import of bulk drugs was ₹39,632 Crore and ₹37,722 Crore respectively.
- In December 2023, revised pharma manufacturing rules were notified under schedule-M relating to Good Manufacturing Practices, a mandatory requirement that safeguards quality and brings the existing regime in line with global standards.
- Recently Govt. has introduced Aatmanirbharta Pursuit which aims to boost domestic manufacturing and Pradhan Mantri Bhartiya Janaushadhi Pariyojana which aims to make quality generic medicines available at affordable prices to all.

Q21. What is the state of India's Infrastructure?

Ans. The state of India's Infrastructure can be discussed ads following:

I. Physical Infrastructure

- **Roads:** The average pace of NH construction increased by about 3 times between FY14 and FY24. Toll digitisation reduced waiting time at toll plazas by nearly 16 times during 2014–24.
- **Railway:** Capital expenditure on Railways increased by 77% per cent between FY20 and FY24. Significant investments in new lines, gauge conversion and doubling.
- **Water Transport:** India's rank in International Shipments category in Logistics Performance Index improved from 44 in 2014 to 22 in 2023.
- **Civil Aviation:** New terminal buildings at 21 airports in FY24. Increase in passenger handling capacity by 62 million passengers per annum.

II. Energy

- **Electrical Power:** India targets 50% of cumulative power installed capacity from non-fossil fuel-based energy sources by 2030.
- **Renewables:** UJALA Scheme led to annual energy savings of 48.42 billion kWh and annual savings of ₹19,335 crore in electricity bills.

III. Urban Sector

- PMAY-U: >1.18 crore houses were sanctioned and more than 84 lakh completed.
- AMRUT Mission: 5,999 projects worth ₹83,327 crore awarded. 5,304 projects worth ₹51,434 crore got completed.
- Metro rail/RRTS: 945 km are operational. 939 km under construction in 27 cities. 86 km operationalised in FY24.
- Swatch Bharat Mission-Urban: Constructed 63.07 lakh individual household latrine units. 6.37 lakh community & public toilets.

IV. Social and Economic Infrastructure

- **Sports:** Khelo India: In FY24, 38 new infrastructure projects were sanctioned; 58 completed. Sports Authority of India: approved 9 infra projects in FY24. 13 completed.
- **Water & Sanitation:** Swatch Bharat Mission-Gramin: In FY24, ₹6,802.6 crore uitilised. Jal Jeevan Mission: Tap water connection provided to more than 14.89 crore rural households so far.
- **Water Resource Management:** Namami Gange: Adopted Hybrid Annuity Model for sewage treatment plants; 33 projects sanctioned. Accelerated Irrigation Benefit Programme: 25.80 lakh hectare of additional irrigation area created during 2016–24.
- **Tourism:** PRASHAD scheme: 29 new pilgrimage and heritage sites identified. Swadesh Darshan 2.0: Outlay of ₹3,800 crore.
- **Space:** India has 55 active space assets, including18 communication satellites, 9 navigation satellites, 5 scientific satellites, 3 meteorological satellites, and 20 earth observation satellites.
- **Telecom:** 8.02 lakh mobile towers as of June 2024. 29.37 lakh Base Transceiver Stations (BTSs) & 4.5 lakh 5G BTSs. BharatNet Project: 6,85,501 km of optical fibre cable (OFC) laid. 2.11 lakh GPs connected by OFC.
- **Electronics & IT:** >₹10,300 crore for comprehensive India Al Mission approved. AIRAWAT, an AI Supercomputer, secured 75th position in the top 500 global supercomputing list declared at the International Supercomputing Conference 2023 in Germany. DigiLocker platform has reached over 26.28 crore registered users.

Q22. What is National Infrastructure Pipeline (NIP)?

Ans. The Government launched the NIP with a projected infrastructure investment of around ₹111 lakh crore during FY20–25 to provide high quality infrastructure across the country. It includes infrastructure projects of more than ₹100 crore each covering greenfield and brownfield investments. The transportation sector dominates with a contribution of 58 per cent, followed by the energy sector at 24 per cent, and the water and sanitation sector at 12 per cent, and balance five per cent by other sectors such as social infrastructure, communication, etc. NIP currently has over 9,666 projects, out of these projects, 4,413 projects (46 per cent) are under implementation.

Q23. Write a note on private sector participation in Space Sector?

Ans. Space sector reforms announced in 2020 were introduced in the participation of private players in the Indian space programme. Some key initiatives are:

- Indian National Space Promotion and Authorisation Centre (IN-SPACe) – a single window agency to promote and authorise space activities was inaugurated in June 2022 at Ahmedabad.
- 51 MoUs and 34 joint project implementation plans have been signed with various non-governmental entities.
- Several entities in the private sector have developed satellites and functional payloads for operations in outer space viz., PixxelSpace, Digantara, Dhruva Space, Azista BST Aerospace, Tata Advanced Systems Limited, etc.

- Launch of Vikram-S (Prarambh mission), a suborbital launch vehicle from M/s Skyroot Aerospace Pvt. Ltd., Hyderabad, in 2022.
- The first private launchpad and mission control centre was established by M/s Agnikul
- Cosmos Pvt. Ltd., Chennai in ISRO campus at SDSC, SHAR in 2022.
- HAL and L&T consortia has been selected as the Indian industry partner for the end-to end production of five PSLVs.
- The process for transfer of small satellite launch vehicle technology has been initiated.

Q24. What is the status of Smart Cities Mission (SCM)?

Ans. SCM was launched in June 2015 to promote cities that provide core infrastructure, clean and sustainable environment and give a decent quality of life to their citizens through the application of 'smart solutions'. A total number of 100 cities have been selected for development as smart cities. As on 20 June 2024, 100 SPVs have undertaken 8,011 multi-sectoral projects worth around ₹1.64 lakh crore; of which 7,153 projects (89 per cent) worth ₹1.43 lakh crore (87 per cent) have been completed.

Q25. What is Atal mission for rejuvenation and urban transformation (AMRUT)?

Ans. AMRUT was launched in June 2015 in 500 cities focused primarily on providing safe and assured drinking water supply universally. Contracts for 5,999 projects worth ₹83,327 crore awarded of which 5,304 projects worth ₹51,434 crore (62 per cent) were completed. AMRUT 2.0 was launched in October 2021 for five years with a focus on making the cities self-reliant & water secure and providing universal coverage of sewerage & septage management in 500 AMRUT cities. Major reforms under AMRUT 2.0 include notification of property tax and user charge, enhancing financial sustainability and water security of urban local bodies, recycle/ reuse of 20 per cent treated used water, double entry accounting system and efficient town planning etc. To encourage PPPs, projects worth 10 per cent of allocation in million plus cities are mandated to be implemented in PPP mode.

REFERENCES

- https://www.indiabudget.gov.in
- https://www.indiabudget.gov.in/economicsurvey
- https://www.india.gov.in/topics/governance
- https://www.india.gov.in/my-government/schemes

UNIT III
CHAPTER-WISE
MULTIPLE-CHOICE QUESTIONS

Chapter 1 Few Basic Concepts and Nature of Indian Economy

1. Consider the following statements. Which of the following is/are false?

I. There is no country in the world at present which is 100% capitalist or socialist

II. India started its march toward capitalism since 1991

III. India was a socialist country at the time of independence

Mark the correct code:

Code:

(a) I only (b) II and III
(c) III only (d) I, II, and III

2. What is true about economic development?

I. It is a continuous process

II. It measures both the quantitative and qualitative aspects of change in national income

III. It is a long-term process

Mark the correct code:

(a) I only (b) II and III
(c) III only (d) I, II, and III

3. Why in India interest rate is high as compared to the United States?

(a) Capital is scarce in India as compared to the United States
(b) RBI deliberately keeps high interest rate as a part of its monetary policy
(c) Money market in India is underdeveloped as compared to that of the United States
(d) All of the above

4. Match the following:

List I	List II
India	Frontier economy
Canada	Developed economy
Myanmar	Less developed country
Argentina	Emerging market

Mark the correct code:

	A	B	C	D
a.	IV	II	III	I
b.	I	II	IV	III
c.	II	III	I	IV
d.	III	I	II	IV

5. What is true about India economy?

I. The dependency ratio of Indian is declining

II. India is experiencing higher proportion of educated unemployment

III. During 2004–2008, the country witnessed an average growth rate reaching an unprecedented high of 8.8% a year

Mark the correct code:

Code:

(a) I and II (b) II and III
(c) Only I (d) I, II, and III

6. Who is the author of "General Theory of Employment Interest and Money"?

(a) J.M. Keynes
(b) J.K. Galbraith
(c) Hansen
(d) Milton Friedman

7. Out of 218 nations classified by World Bank, how many nations are high income economies in 2024?

(a) <50
(b) Between 50 and 75
(c) Between 75 and 100
(d) Between 100 and 125

8. Economic growth is:

(a) Long-term process
(b) Measures both qualitative and quantitative aspects
(c) Discontinuous process
(d) None of the above

9. Who is called the founder of microeconomics?

(a) Adam Smith (b) David Ricardo
(c) J.M. Keynes (d) None of the above

10. What is true about water-diamond paradox?

I. It was given by Adam Smith in his book *Wealth of Nations*
II. Diamond is scarce, so its marginal utility is high, and hence, it is expensive.
III. Diamond is a luxury, water is a necessity, and hence, water is cheaper

Mark the correct code:

Code:

(a) I, II, and III (b) I and III
(c) I and II (d) Only III

Chapter 2 National Income, Savings, and Capital Formation

1. Which of the following statement is true?

I. India is world's third largest economy in terms of purchasing power parity, after China and the United States
II. The Financing, real estate, and professional services constitute largest share among the services
III. In 1970–1971, service sector out surpassed agriculture sector and became largest contributor in India's GDP

Mark the correct code:

Code:

(a) I and II (b) II and III
(c) III only (d) I only

2. Which of the following statement is true with regard to gross value added (GVA)?

I. The concept of GVA was introduced by CSO in the year 2013
II. GVA at basic prices is GDP at market prices minus product taxes plus product subsidies
III. The concept of GVA follows from the United Nation's System of National Accounts (SNA) introduced in 1993 and revised in 2008

Mark the correct code:

Code:

(a) I and III (b) II and III
(c) Only III (d) I, II and III

3. What is the approximate share of private corporate sector in total savings of the nation?

(a) 74% (b) 58%
(c) 45% (d) 35%

4. What is true regarding national income at constant prices?

(a) If goods and services produced in a year are valued at the prices of the base year, we get national income at constant prices
(b) It is also called real national income
(c) It is better method of measuring national it takes into consideration changes in physical output while ignoring prices factor
(d) All of the above

5. In technical sense, the national income is ______.

(a) GDP at MP (b) NNP at MP
(c) GNP at FC (d) NNP at FC

6. What was the achieved growth rate of 12th five-year plan (2012–2017)?

(a) 5.4% (b) 6.8%
(c) 7.5% (d) 8.3%

7. Which state has the highest per capita income in India?

(a) Maharashtra (b) Gujarat
(c) Goa (d) Haryana

8. What is true with regard to gross domestic capital formation in India?

I. The approximate value of ICOR in the country at present is less than 3%
II. The rate of capital formation in India has witnessed an increasing trend during post-reform period
III. In India the rate of gross capital formation remained less for a larger period of time since independence

Mark the correct code:

Code:

(a) I, II and III
(b) II and III
(c) I and II
(d) Only III

9. Who gave the concept of Hindu rate of growth?

(a) Raj Krishna
(b) Dadabhai Naoroji
(c) Arvind Subramanian
(d) Kaushik Basu

10. Match the following:

Sector	Approximate Share in GDP (2017–2018)
A. Mining & Quarrying	I. 15%
B. Agriculture	II. 3%
C. Construction	III. 18%
D. Manufacturing	IV. 8%

Mark the correct code:

	A	B	C	D
a.	I	II	III	IV
b.	IV	II	III	I
c.	II	I	IV	III
d.	I	II	IV	III

Chapter 3 Human Development and Happiness Economics

1. Geometric mean is used to calculate HDI because:

(a) Poor performance in any dimension is directly reflected in the geometric mean
(b) It is simpler method than arithmetic mean
(c) It lowers the impact of income
(d) It increases the level of substitutability between dimensions

2. All the dimensions of HDI for India have _______ since 1990.

(a) decreased
(b) increased
(c) remained same
(d) first increased then decreased

3. What of the following statement is untrue?

(a) HDI can be disaggregated by gender, ethnic group, or geographical region
(b) GNP is single dimension whereas HDI is multi-dimensional
(c) The success story of East Asian nations reveals that high income levels, by themselves, are guarantee for human progress
(d) Human development gaps between the nations are more manageable than widening income disparities

4. IHDI was introduced by:

(a) HDR 1990 (b) HDR 1997
(c) HDR 2010 (d) HDR 2014

5. The Gender Inequality Index (GII) reflects women's disadvantages in three dimensions. They are reproductive health, empowerment, and _______.

(a) education
(b) malnutrition
(c) maternal mortality
(d) economic activity

6. There are six indicators under "Standard of Living" dimension of MPI. Which one of them is not the correct indicator?

(a) sanitation
(b) electricity
(c) housing
(d) per capita income above US $5,000 p.a. (in terms of PPP)

7. Under GDI, the dimension of health is measured by:

I. female and male life expectancy at birth
II. female and male malnutrition
III. female and male child mortality

Please mark the correct code:

(a) I and II (b) II only
(c) I, II, and III (d) I only

8. The Gross National Happiness propounded by Bhutan in 1972 comprises four variables. Which one of them is not the correct variable?

(a) spiritual development
(b) preservation and promotion of cultural values
(c) conservation of natural environment
(d) establishment of good governance

9. Six factors are used to predict happiness across the nations as per world happiness report. Which one of them is not the correct factor?

(a) life expectancy (b) generosity
(c) gratitude (d) freedom

10. Easterlin paradox explains:

(a) positive correlation between income and happiness
(b) positive correlation between health and happiness
(c) increase in subjective well-being as income continues to grow
(d) decrease in subjective well-being as income continues to grow

Chapter 4 Natural Resources, Environment, and Sustainable Development

1. Arable land in the irrigated zones of India is turning saline due to which of the following reasons?

(a) Addition of gypsum
(b) Over irrigation
(c) Over grazing
(d) Use of fertilizers

2. Which state ranks first in mineral production?

(a) Jharkhand
(b) West Bengal
(c) Odisha
(d) Rajasthan

3. Match the following:

List I	List II
A. Earth Summit	I. 1992
B. Rio + 10	II. 2002
C. Rio + 20	III. 2012
D. UN Sustainable Development Summit	IV. 2015

Mark the correct code:

	A	B	C	D
a.	I	II	III	IV
b.	IV	II	III	I
c.	II	III	I	IV
d.	III	I	II	IV

4. Which of the following statement(s) is/are true?

I. In India, arable land constitutes more than 50% of total geographical area
II. Alluvial soils cover around 40% of the area of the country
III. Indian Agriculture Research Institute is located in Kanpur

Mark the correct code:

Code:

(a) I and II (b) II and III
(c) Only II (d) I, II, and III

5. Which of the following statement(s) is/are true?

(a) India accounts for 1% of global forest area
(b) Among states, Arunachal Pradesh has the maximum forest area
(c) As a percentage of state's geographical area Mizoram has the highest forest cover

Mark the correct code:

Code:

(a) I, II, and III (b) II and III
(c) I and III (d) Only III

6. Who is credited with first explaining the term "sustainable development"?

(a) Rachel Carson
(b) Brundtland Commission

(c) United Nations Environment Program
(d) None of the above

7. Which of the following is not the constituent of Paris Agreement?

I. A long-term goal of keeping the increase in global average temperature to well below 2°C above pre-industrial levels
II. India has refused to confirm to "Nationally Determined Contributions" outlined in Paris Agreement
III. The participating nations agreed to bring down greenhouse emissions by 25%

Mark the correct code:

Code:

(a) I, II, and III (b) II and III
(c) I and II (d) Only III

8. Which state has secured the first rank in Composite Water Management Index?

(a) Gujarat (b) Maharashtra
(c) Andhra Pradesh (d) Goa

9. Match the following:

List I	List II
A. National Green Highways Mission	I. 2013
B. National Green Corridor Program	II. 2008
C. National Action Plan on Climate Change	III. 2015
D. FAME India	

Mark the correct code:

	A	B	C	D
a.	I	II	III	II
b.	III	II	II	I
c.	III	I	II	III
d.	I	II	III	I

10. In which year National Air Quality Index was launched?

(a) 2011 (b) 2013
(c) 2015 (d) 2017

Chapter 5 Indian Infrastructure

1. Which of the following statement(s) is/are true about Indian Railways?

I. The first passenger line was opened in 1857 connecting the port of Bombay to Thana
II. Indian Railways is divided into 16 zones that are further sub-divided into 73 divisions
III. Congestion takes place because of lack of multiple tracks and common corridor for both freight and passenger traffic

Mark the correct code:

Code:

(a) I and III (b) II and III
(c) II only (d) III only

2. Which of the following statement(s) is/ are true about conventional energy in India?

I. Coal is one of the primary sources of energy, accounting for about 67% of the total energy consumption in the country
II. India's first hydropower generation plant on Ganga River at Rudraprayag became operational in 1897
III. The development of Natural Gas industry in the country started in 1960s with discovery of gas fields in Assam and Gujarat

Mark the correct code:

Code:

(a) I and III
(b) II and III
(c) III Only
(d) I, II, and III

3. In which year National Solar Mission was launched?

(a) 1999 (b) 2010
(c) 2014 (d) 2017

4. **Match the following:**

List I	List II
A. Doordarshan	I. 1957
B. Vividh Bharati	II. 1959
C. FM Service	III. 1977
D. Postal index number	IV. 1972

Mark the correct code:

	A	B	C	D
a.	I	II	III	IV
b.	II	I	III	IV
c.	II	III	I	IV
d.	I	III	II	IV

5. **Which of the following statement(s) is/are true?**
   I. The approximate share of renewable energy in gross electricity generation is 11%
   II. Agriculture consumes around 40% of energy in India
   III. The estimated potential for power generation in the country from small hydro-plants is 40,000 MW

   Mark the correct code:

   Code:
   (a) I and II
   (b) II and III
   (c) I, II, and III
   (d) None of the above

6. **Which of the following statement(s) is/are true?**
   I. Uttar Pradesh has the largest road network in the country
   II. Maharashtra accounts for the largest share in the total length of National Highways
   III. Kolkata port is the oldest port in the country

   Mark the correct code:

   Code:
   (a) I and II (b) II and III
   (c) I and II (d) III Only

7. **Which is the first major non-governmental port in the country?**
   (a) Jawahar Lal Nehru Port Trust
   (b) Ennore
   (c) Visakhapatnam
   (d) VO Chidambaranar

8. **Which nuclear power plant has the highest installed capacity in the country?**
   (a) Kudankulam (b) Tarapur
   (c) Kaiga (d) Rawatbhata

9. **In which year the Pradhan Mantri Ujjwala Yojana was launched in India?**
   (a) 2014 (b) 2015
   (c) 2016 (d) 2017

10. **Match the following:**

Hydro Project	State
A. Srisailam	I. Andhra Pradesh
B. Nathpa Jhakri	II. Maharashtra
C. Indira Sagar	III. Himachal Pradesh
D. Koyna	IV. Madhya Pradesh

Mark the correct code:

	A	B	C	D
a.	I	II	III	IV
b.	IV	II	III	I
c.	II	I	III	IV
d.	I	III	IV	II

Chapter 6 India's Population and Demographic Dividend

1. **Which year is called the year of great divide?**
   (a) 1921 (b) 1951
   (c) 1991 (d) 2001

2. **Which of the following statement(s) is/are true?**
   I. The share of Hindu population has decreased since independence.

II. The percentage share of Christian population has remained constant since independence.
III. The Muslims constitute nearly 14% of the entire population in the country.

Mark the correct code:

Code:

(a) I and III (b) II and III
(c) Only III (d) I, II, and III

3. What is the share of Uttar Pradesh in the total population in the country as per census 2011?

(a) 21.63% (b) 19.23%
(c) 16.49% (d) 13.33%

4. Match the following:

List I	List II
A. ASHA	I. Birth spacing
B. Santushti	II. Sterilization
C. Prerna	III. Health worker
D. Jansankhya Sthirata Kosh	IV. Raising contributions

Mark the correct code:

	A	B	C	D
a.	I	II	III	IV
b.	IV	II	III	I
c.	II	III	I	IV
d.	III	II	I	IV

5. Which of the following statement(s) is/are untrue?

(a) Asia will be the largest contributor to the world population during 2017–2050 followed by Africa
(b) India has 2.4% of the world's total area and the home for nearly 17.5% of the world population
(c) Proportion of economically active population (15–59 years) is 62.5% as per census 2011
(d) Haryana has the lowest sex ratio in the country as per census 2011

6. Which of the following may retard tapping of demographic dividend in India?

I. Lesser women participation in jobs reflecting lower LFPR.
II. Large-scale informal employment that mars the productivity of Indian workers.
III. Massive unskilled population

Mark the correct code:

Code:

(a) I, II, and III
(b) II and III
(c) I and II
(d) Only III

7. The fourth stage of demographic transition is characterized by ________.

(a) both birth rate and death rate fall but the fall in death rate is steeper
(b) both birth rate and death rate fall but the fall in birth rate is steeper
(c) Stationery population growth
(d) None of the above

8. Which of the following statement(s) is/are true with regard to National Population Policy (NPP), 2000?

I. The "long-term objective" of NPP is to achieve a stable population by 2045.
II. The policy emphasizes freezing the number of seats in Lok Sabha at the current level of 543, which is based on the 1971 census till 2026.
III. Reduce infant mortality rate to below 30 per 1,000 live births and maternal mortality rate to below 100 per 1,00,000 live births by the year 2010.

Mark the correct code:

Code:

(a) I, II, and III
(b) II and III
(c) I and II
(d) Only III

9. Who headed an expert group on National Population Policy in 1993?

(a) M.S. Swaminathan
(b) Montek Singh Ahluwalia
(c) Sam Pitroda
(d) Jaswant Singh

10. In which year the first all India census was completed?

(a) 1851 (b) 1872
(c) 1901 (d) 1911

Chapter 7 Poverty and Inequality in India

1. Which country in Europe became first to launch and experiment universal basic income for 2 years on pilot basis on January 1, 2017?

(a) England (b) Sweden
(c) Norway (d) Finland

2. What are the estimates for rural poverty according to Rangarajan committee in 2011?

(a) 30.9 (b) 26.4
(c) 29.5 (d) 27.5

3. What is untrue regarding policies to eliminate poverty?

I. Poverty alleviation measures were adopted immediately after independence in India.
II. Wage employment and skill development programs were introduced during 12th 5-year plan.
III. Post-reform period focused on trickle down approach to eliminate poverty.

Mark the correct code:

Code:

(a) I, II, and III (b) II and III
(c) I and III (d) Only II

4. Match the following:

List I	List II
A. Tendulkar committee	I. 1977
B. Alagh committee	II. 1989
C. Rangarajan committee	III. 2005
D. Lakdawala committee	IV. 2012

Mark the correct code:

	A	B	C	D
a.	I	II	III	IV
b.	II	I	IV	III
c.	II	III	I	IV
d.	III	I	IV	II

5. Which of the following is not the indicator to measure the dimension of standard of living in multi-dimensional poverty index?

(a) Cooking fuel (b) Floor
(c) Literacy (d) Toilet

6. What is the newly revised average calorie requirement as per C. Rangarajan committee?

(a) 2,400 kcal per capita per day in rural areas and 2,100 kcal per capita per day in urban areas
(b) 2,285 kcal per capita per day in rural areas and 1,995 kcal per capita per day in urban areas
(c) 2,155 kcal per capita per day in rural areas and 2,090 kcal per capita per day in urban areas
(d) 2,300 kcal per capita per day in rural areas and 2,080 kcal per capita per day in urban areas

7. Match the following:

List I	List II
A. Tendulkar committee	I. Uniform recall period
B. Alagh committee	II. Mixed recall period
C. Rangarajan committee	III. Modified Mixed Recall Period
D. Lakdawala committee	

Mark the correct code:

	A	B	C	D
a.	I	II	III	I
b.	II	I	III	I
c.	II	III	I	II
d.	III	I	II	I

8. Who gave the concept of poverty line in India based on calorie norms?

(a) B.S. Minhas (b) Alagh committee
(c) Manmohan Singh (d) M.S. Ahluwalia

9. What is the rank of India in Gender Inequality Index as per HDR 2018?

(a) 117 (b) 127
(c) 137 (d) 147

10. Which of the following can be attributed as main cause of inequality in India?

(a) Crony capitalism
(b) Inherited wealth
(c) Gender bias
(d) All of the above

Chapter 8 Labor Force, Occupational Pattern, and Unemployment in India

1. What is true about MGNREGS?

I. Providing not less than 100 days of guaranteed employment in a financial year.

II. Wage rates for workers under the scheme are notified and revised annually based on WPI.

III. 60 : 40 wage and material ratio for permissible works.

Mark the correct code:

Code:

(a) I and III (b) II and III
(c) III only (d) I, II, and III

2. In which year Pradhan Mantri Kaushal Vikas Yojana was launched?

(a) 2014 (b) 2015
(c) 2016 (d) 2017

3. Which approach to measure unemployment is most relevant for policymaking as it is more inclusive and covers both open as well as partial unemployment?

(a) Usual principal status
(b) Usual status
(c) Current weekly status
(d) Current daily status

4. Match the following:

List I	List II
A. People move between jobs	I. Disguised unemployment
B. Amusement parks during winter	II. Frictional unemployment
C. Technological shifts	III. Structural unemployment
D. Zero marginal productivity	IV. Seasonal Unemployment

Mark the correct code:

	A	B	C	D
a.	I	II	IV	III
b.	I	II	IV	III
c.	II	IV	III	I
d.	III	I	II	IV

5. What explains jobless growth syndrome in India?

I. Growth in services is not matched by commensurate growth in employment.

II. There is lack of skilled workforce in India.

III. Labor absorption is less in industry and services sector.

Mark the correct code:

Code:

(a) I and II (b) II and III
(c) Only I (d) I, II, and III

6. Match the following:

List I	List II
A. SGSY	I. 1993
B. NREP	II. 1999
C. NRLM	III. 2011
D. EAS	IV. 1980

Mark the correct code:

	A	B	C	D
a.	I	II	IV	III
b.	I	II	IV	III
c.	II	IV	III	I
d.	III	I	II	IV

7. Which factor is responsible for declining labor force participation rate during recent years?

(a) Women prefer to stay at home
(b) Women seeking education and skill
(c) Lack of opportunities for women
(d) None of the above

8. Which of the following statement is not true?

(a) The public sector has retired more employees than it recruited during the post-reform period.

(b) Among states, Kerala had the lowest unemployment rate in India in 2011.

(c) The overall proportion of informal workers in total employment is around 92%.

(d) Unemployment rate is highest under current daily status approach.

9. What is the share of industrial employment in 2011 as per NSSO 68th round?

(a) 29.4 (b) 24.4
(c) 31.4 (d) 19.4

10. Which of the following statement(s) is/are true?

I. Main workers are those workers who had worked for major part of the reference period.
II. In India, male workers have always accounted for more than two-third of Indian labor force.
III. The incidence of child labor has decreased between 2001 and 2011.

Mark the correct code:

Code:
(a) I and II (b) II and III
(c) Only I (d) I, II, and III

Chapter 9 Indian Economy During Pre-independence Period

1. What is true about Arthashastra, a great Indian ancient manuscript?

I. It deals in effective economic and political governance.
II. Arthashastra was first translated in English in the year 1904.
III. It influenced the Mughal and colonial economic and political polices in India.

Mark the correct code:

Code:
(a) I and II (b) II and III
(c) I only (d) I, II, and III

2. Who authored the book "Poverty and Un-British Rule in India"?

(a) A.O. Hume
(b) R.C. Dutt
(c) Dadabhai Naoroji
(d) M.G. Ranade

3. Which event marks the watershed as far as the establishment of colonial rule in India is concerned?

(a) Establishment of East India Company in 1600
(b) Battle of Plassey in 1757
(c) Sepoy Mutiny in 1857
(d) Permanent Settlement in Bengal in 1793

4. Who has authored the book "An era of darkness"?

(a) Shashi Tharoor
(b) Arundhati Roy
(c) Angus Maddison
(d) Jawaharlal Nehru

5. What facilitated commercialization of agriculture in India?

I. Opening of Suez Canal
II. Introduction of money
III. American Civil War

Mark the correct code:

Code:
(a) I and II
(b) II and III
(c) I, II, and III
(d) None of the above

6. Match the following:

List I	List II
A. Alexandor Dow	I. Drain of wealth
B. Lord Macaulay	II. Minutes to Education
C. Lord Cornwallis	III. Zamindari System
D. R.C. Dutt	

Mark the correct code:

	A	B	C	D
a.	I	II	IV	III
b.	I	II	IV	III
c.	II	IV	III	I
d.	I	II	III	I

7. Which of the following statement(s) is/are true?

I. India's first railway line was opened in Madras in 1837.
II. The first jute mill was built in 1854.
III. First Indian steel mill was built in 1911.

Mark the correct code:

Code:

(a) I and II (b) II and III
(c) I, II, and III (d) III only

8. Which out of following was not contributory factor to the "drain of wealth" in India?

(a) Transfer of income from private trade or investment
(b) Home charges
(c) Commercialization of agriculture
(d) Remittances

9. What caused deindustrialization in India during colonial rule?

I. Increase in wages in India
II. Increased competitiveness of British textiles
III. Increase in transport facility

Mark the correct code:

Code:

(a) I and II (b) II only
(c) I, II, and III (d) II and III

10. Which of the following statement(s) is/are true?

I. Per capita GDP of India was more than that of the United Kingdom during 1600 A.D.
II. India's per capita income from 1600–1947 increased by 12%, whereas the increase for Britain for the same period was more than 500%.
III. India's population during 1600 A.D. was less than that of Britain.

Mark the correct code:

Code:

(a) I and II (b) II and III
(c) Only II (d) I, II, and III

Chapter 10 Indian Agriculture: Productivity, Land Reforms, and Livestock

1. What is true about Indian agriculture?

I. The share of agriculture in the country's GVA has declined since independence.
II. The Kharif cropping season is from October to March (winter) and the Rabi cropping season is July to October (during the south-west monsoon)
III. The growth rate of agriculture has become consistent during the post-reform period.

Mark the correct code:

Code:

(a) I and II (b) II and III
(c) III only (d) I only

2. Which of the following is/are the cause(s) of low agriculture productivity in India?

I. Fragmented landholdings
II. Inadequate access to credit and insurance
III. Low arable land as compared to China and the United States

Mark the correct code:

Code:

(a) I and II (b) II and III
(c) Only III (d) Only II

3. Which of the following is not the component of land reforms in India?

(a) Regulation of agriculture Mandis
(b) Conferment of ownership rights to the tenants
(c) Cooperative farming
(d) Land distribution among the agricultural laborers

4. Match the following:

List I	List II
A. Soil health card scheme	I. 2013
B. Agriculture export policy	II. 2018
C. Operation Barga	III. 1978
D. National livestock policy	IV. 2015

Mark the correct code:

	A	B	C	D
a.	I	II	III	IV
b.	IV	II	III	I
c.	II	III	I	IV
d.	III	I	II	IV

5. Which of the following statement(s) is/are true?

I. In India's Agriculture import expenditure, Edible oil is the largest import item.
II. In India, food grains are grown on nearly 75% of gross cropped area and wheat is grown on nearly on 34% of total area.
III. GCF in agriculture has revealed a declining trend during 1991 to 2014 and exhibited a rising trend in recent years.

Mark the correct code:

Code:

(a) I and III (b) II and III
(c) Only III (d) I, II, and III

6. Which of the following statement(s) is/are not true regarding soil health card scheme?

I. It was introduced in the year 2015.
II. It educates farmers regarding soil health on the basis of 12 parameters.
III. The scheme is available to only small and marginal farmers.

Mark the correct code:

Code:

(a) I, II, and III (b) II and III
(c) I and II (d) Only III

7. Government of India has given the vision to double farmers' income by the year ________.

(a) 2025 (b) 2022
(c) 2030 (d) 2024

8. Which of the following statement(s) is/are not true?

(a) India is the second largest producer of milk in the world
(b) India has the world's largest stock of cattle and buffaloes
(c) The marginal farm households control more than half of country's cattle and buffalo
(d) Government has extended the facility of the Kisan credit cards and insurance to the livestock sector

9. In which state operation Barga was launched?

(a) Kerala (b) Bihar
(c) Gujarat (d) West Bengal

10. What is true about India's livestock sector?

I. Women constitute about 69% of workforce in livestock sector.
II. Livestock sector contributes 4.5% of country's GVA and nearly 26% of agriculture GVA.
III. The National Livestock Mission (NLM) was launched in 2014–2015.

Mark the correct code:

Code:

(a) I, II, and III (b) II and III
(c) Only I (d) Only II

Chapter 11 Agriculture Inputs and Green Revolution

1. Which of the following statement (s) is/are true?

I. Nutrient-based subsidy (NBS) scheme was launched on April 1, 2010.
II. China is the top country by fertilizer consumption in the world.
III. India imports 100% of its potassic fertilizers from abroad.

Mark the correct code:

Code:

(a) I and III (b) II and III
(c) III only (d) I only

2. Which of the following statement (s) is/are true?

I. FDI is permitted up to 100% under the automatic route in the development and production of seeds and planting material subject to certain conditions.
II. The Central Insecticides Laboratory has been established at Faridabad.
III. The Integrated Pest Management scheme was launched by GOI in 1985.

Mark the correct code:

Code:

(a) I and III (b) II and III
(c) Only III (d) I, II, and III

3. What is the approximate share of canal irrigation as a percentage of total irrigation in the country?

(a) 19% (b) 26%
(c) 35% (d) 61%

4. Match the following:

List I	List II
A. Pradhan Mantri Krishi Sinchayee Yojana	I. 2015
B. National Mission on Micro Irrigation	II. 2010
C. Green Revolution	III. 1966
D. City compost scheme	IV. 2016

Mark the correct code:

	A	B	C	D
a.	I	II	III	IV
b.	IV	II	III	I
c.	II	III	I	IV
d.	III	I	II	IV

5. What is true about Green Revolution in India?

I. Green Revolution was launched in the Rabi season of 1966.
II. M.S. Randhawa is called the father of Green Revolution in Punjab.
II. Green Revolution started spreading to other parts of the country since the year 1991.

Mark the correct code:

Code:

(a) I and II (b) II and III
(c) Only II (d) I, II, and III

6. Which of the following statement (s) is/are not true?

I. Bt Brinjal was introduced to Indian farmers in 2008.
II. The International Rice Research Institute is established in Bhopal.
III. Lerma Rojo 64 is a HYV seed variety of wheat.

Mark the correct code:

Code:

(a) I, II, and III (b) II and III
(c) I and II (d) Only III

7. Which of the following does not constitute strategies for second Green Revolution in India?

(a) Thrust on biotechnology
(b) Livestock development
(c) Agroforestry
(d) Loan waiver of farmers

8. Which of the following statement is true with regard to negative impact of Green Revolution in India?

I. The Green Revolution was crop specific and region specific, and created interpersonal and regional inequalities.
II. The use of HYV seeds displaced indigenous species and agricultural system that had been built up over generations.
III. The in-migration of labor is believed to have depressed wage rate of labor in Punjab.

Mark the correct code:

Code:

(a) I, II, and III (b) II and III
(c) I and II (d) Only III

9. Who gave the concept of virtual water?

(a) Sir William Gaud
(b) John Anthony Allan
(c) Sam Pitroda
(d) M.S. Swaminathan

10. Match the following:

List I	List II
A. Pink Revolution	I. Meat
B. Silver	II. Egg
C. Brown Revolution	III. Horticulture
D. Golden Revolution	IV. Cocoa

Mark the correct code:

	A	B	C	D
a.	I	II	III	IV
b.	IV	II	III	I
c.	II	III	I	IV
d.	I	II	IV	III

Chapter 12 Agriculture Prices and Food Security

1. Which of the following statement(s) is/are untrue?

I. Agriculture Price Commission (APC) was established in 1965 and renamed as Commission for Agriculture Cost and Prices (CACP) in 1985.
II. APC was established on the recommendations of M.S. Swaminathan committee.
III. A2 costs are the costs that the farmer incurs for buying various inputs such as seeds, fertilizers, fertilizers, hired/owned labor, hired/owned machinery, and rent paid for leased land.

Mark the correct code:

Code:

(a) I and III (b) II and III
(c) II only (d) I only

2. Which of the following statement(s) is/are true?

I. There is open-ended purchase and sale policy for wheat, rice, and pulses in the country.
II. Procurement price is the price at which the Government sells foodgrains to general public at subsidized prices.
III. Buffer stocks serve as shock absorbers in the economy and provide a defense mechanism against widely fluctuating price levels.

Mark the correct code:

Code:

(a) I and III (b) II and III
(c) Only III (d) I, II and III

3. In which year FCI was set up in the country?

(a) 1957 (b) 1960
(c) 1965 (d) 1968

4. Match the following:

List I	List II
A. AAY	I. 2000
B. TPDS	II. 2013
C. NFSA	III. 1997
D. ICDS	IV. 1975

Mark the correct code:

	A	B	C	D
a.	I	II	III	IV
b.	IV	II	III	I
c.	II	III	I	IV
d.	I	III	II	IV

5. What is true about PDS in India?

I. PDS was first launched in Bombay in 1939.
II. The Central Government takes the responsibility for procurement, storage, transportation, and allocation, whereas the state governments take the operational responsibility of PDS.
III. Revamped PDS was launched in 1992.

Mark the correct code:

Code:

(a) I and II (b) II and III
(c) Only II (d) I, II and III

6. Which of the following is not the advantage of MSP policy in India?

I. Announcement of MSP has led to adoption of technology by farmers.
II. MSP policy has provided income stability to the farmers.
III. MSP policy has promoted regional equality in India.

Mark the correct code:

Code:

(a) I and II (b) II and III
(c) I and II (d) Only III

7. Which of the following is not the indicator of Global Hunger Index?

(a) Child wasting
(b) Child stunting
(c) Undernourishment
(d) Starvation

8. Which of the following statement(s) is/are true with regard to food security in India?

I. The per capita consumption of cereals has decreased in India but that of protein-rich items has increased.

II. India is the home for highest number of poor, hungry, malnourished, and anemic people in the world.
III. The per capita availability of foodgrains has experienced a fluctuating trend since 1951.

Mark the correct code:

Code:

(a) I, II and III (b) II and III
(c) I and II (d) Only III

9. Which of the following can be cited as the cause of rising food subsidy bill?

(a) Increase in issue price
(b) PDS leakages
(c) Increase in MSP
(d) Low procurement and offtake of foodgrains

10. Match the following:

List I	List II
A. NFSA	I. School enrolment and nutrition
B. Mid-Day Meal	II. Legal entitlement
C. ICDS	III. Early childhood care and development
D. Antyodaya Ann Yojana	VI. Poorest of poor

Mark the correct code:

	A	B	C	D
a.	I	II	III	IV
b.	IV	II	III	I
c.	II	I	III	IV
d.	I	II	IV	III

Chapter 13 Agriculture Finance in India

1. In the last six decades, the share of commercial banks in agriculture credit has increased dramatically because of the following:

I. Lead Bank Scheme
II. Service area approach
III. Priority sector lending

Mark the correct code:

Code:

(a) I and II (b) I and III
(c) I, II and III (d) II and III

2. What is true about Pradhan Mantri Fasal Bima Yojana?

I. It was launched in February 2016.
II. A uniform premium of only 2% to be paid by farmers for all Kharif and Rabi crops.
III. All other schemes like Restructured Weather Based Crop Insurance Scheme, Unified Package Insurance Scheme, and Coconut Palm Insurance Scheme have been subsumed under this scheme.

Mark the correct code:

Code:

(a) I and III (b) II and III
(c) Only III (d) Only I

3. What is true about NABARD?

(a) NABARD provides direct finance to the farmers
(b) NABARD is empowered to conduct inspection of agriculture lending by commercial banks
(c) NABARD is fully owned by RBI
(d) Long-term irrigation fund was created with NABARD in 2017

4. Match the following:

List I	List II
A. NABARD	I. 2015
B. Regional Rural Banks	II. 1982
C. Eshakti	III. 1975
D. Kisan Credit Card	IV. 1998

Mark the correct code:

	A	B	C	D
a.	I	II	III	IV
b.	II	I	IV	III
c.	II	III	I	IV
d.	III	I	II	IV

5. What is true about Rural Infrastructure Development Fund (RIDF)?

I. It was established with NABARD in 1995–1996.
II. Shortfall in lending to priority sector by scheduled commercial banks is credited into RIDF.
III. The major beneficiaries of RIDF are State Governments, gram panchayats, self-help groups, and NGOs.

Mark the correct code:

Code:

(a) I, II and III (b) II and III
(c) Only III (d) Only II

6. What is true about farmers' suicide in India?

I. The yearly number of suicides has gone up during the recent years.
II. The major cause of farmers' suicide is crop failure.
III. The states which have weak financial institutional system have witnessed larger number of farm suicides.

Mark the correct code:

Code:

(a) I, II and III
(b) II and III
(c) I and III
(d) None of the above.

7. In which year the Coconut Palm Insurance Scheme was launched?

(a) 2009 (b) 2012
(c) 2014 (d) 2016

8. Which of the following is not a probable implication of farm loan waivers?

(a) It infuses credit indiscipline among farmers.
(b) It increases NPAs of the banks in the eventuality of staggered repayments by the state.
(c) It encourages farmer lobbying in the political circles.
(d) It does not affect the fiscal deficit of the states as such states are compensated by the Central Government.

9. In which year interest subvention scheme was launched by Government of India?

(a) 2006–2007 (b) 2009–2010
(c) 2015–2016 (d) 2017–2018

10. Which of the following recommendation(s) was/were made by National commission on farmers headed by M.S. Swaminathan in its report on farmers' distress?

I. MSP should be at least 50% more than the weighted average cost of production.
II. Issuing Kisan Credit Cards to women farmers.
III. Ensuring grazing rights and seasonal access to forests to tribals and pastoralists.

Mark the correct code:

Code:

(a) I, II and III (b) II and III
(c) Only I (d) Only II

Chapter 14 Agriculture Marketing in India

1. What is true about NAM?

I. It is pan-Indian non-electronic trading portal.
II. It was launched in 2016.
III. NAM helps remove information asymmetry among buyers and sellers.

Mark the correct code:

Code:

(a) I and II (b) I and III
(c) I, II, and III (d) II and III

2. The Model Agriculture Produce and Livestock Contract Farming and Services (Promotion & Facilitation) Act, 2018 does not envisage

I. Contracted produce is to be covered under crop/livestock insurance in operation.
II. Contract framing will not be outside the ambit of APMC Act.
III. Among the farmer and firm, the farmer is considered as a weaker party.

Mark the correct code:

Code:

(a) I and III (b) II and III
(c) Only III (d) Only II

3. What is untrue about Agriculture Price Market Committee (APMC)?

(a) Agricultural markets are established and regulated by state APMC Act
(b) APMCs generally consist of representatives of farmers, traders, warehousing entities, registrar of co-operative societies, etc
(c) APMCs charge multiple levies and taxes
(d) Under APMC Act, the whole state is considered as one geographical area and a single unit

4. Match the following

List I	List II
A. Central Warehousing corporation	I. 1988
B. National Institute of Agricultural Marketing	II. 1957
C. Small Farmers' agribusiness consortium	III. 1937
D. Agricultural Produce (Grading and Marketing) Act	IV. 1994

Mark the correct code:

	A	B	C	D
a.	I	II	III	IV
b.	II	I	IV	III
c.	II	III	I	IV
d.	III	I	II	IV

5. What is true about Agricultural Marketing and Farmer Friendly Reforms Index (AMFFRI)?

I. It has been constructed by NABARD.
II. One of the variables of AMFFRI is liberalization of land lease.
III. All states (except UTs) are covered under AMFFRI.

Mark the correct code:

Code:

(a) I and III (b) II and III
(c) Only III (d) Only II

6. What is true about Agricultural Produce and Livestock Marketing (Promotion & Facilitation) Act, 2017?

I. It replaced APMC Act, 2003.
II. It promotes e-trading of agriculture produce.
III. It rationalizes market fee and commission charges.

Mark the correct code:

Code:

(a) I, II, and III (b) II and III
(c) I and III (d) Only II

7. In which year NAFED was established?

(a) 1948 (b) 1958
(c) 1968 (d) 1978

8. Which of the following statement(s) is/are not true?

(a) Agriculture marketing is a state subject.
(b) Rural primary markets are the periodical markets.
(c) Terminal markets are new experiment in India.
(d) Big Bazaar is the example of wholesale market.

9. Central AGMARK laboratory is located at

(a) Nagpur
(b) Faridabad
(c) Chandigarh
(d) Mysore

10. What is true with regard to FSSAI?

I. It was created in 2008.
II. It covers only agriculture food items.
III. FSSAI has replaced AGMARK.

Mark the correct code:

Code:

(a) I, II, and III (b) II and III
(c) Only I (d) Only II

Chapter 15 Industrial Development and Policies

1. What is true about industrial policies in India?

I. The IPR 1956 is hailed as economic constitution of India.
II. Industries (Development and Regulation) Act, 1951 introduced industrial licensing in India.
III. IPR 1977 gave boost to small-scale sector.

Mark the correct code:

Code:

(a) I and II (b) II and III
(c) III only (d) I, II, and III

2. Which committee suggested adoption of new competition law and doing away with MRTP Act?

(a) P. C. Mahalanobis
(b) S. V. S. Raghavan
(c) R. K. Hazari
(d) Subimal Dutt

3. How many sectors have been identified under Make in India campaign of the Government of India?

(a) 15 (b) 25
(c) 35 (d) 40

4. Match the following

List I	List II
A. Make in India	I. 2014
B. National manufacturing policy	II. 2011
C. Mudra scheme	III. 2016
D. Smart city	IV. 2015

Mark the correct code:

	A	B	C	D
a.	I	II	IV	III
b.	IV	II	III	I
c.	II	III	I	IV
d.	III	I	II	IV

5. What is untrue about National Investment Promotion Zones?

I. The central government will provide suitable land having an area of 5,000 ha in size.
II. A special purpose vehicle will be constituted to take care of functioning of the NIMZ.
III. The government has announced eight investment regions along the Delhi Mumbai Industrial Corridor.

Mark the correct code:

Code:

(a) I and II (b) II and III
(c) Only I (d) I, II, and III

6. Which of the following is not the objective of National Manufacturing Policy, 2011?

I. Create 100 million additional jobs by 2022.
II. Create appropriate skill sets among the rural migrant and urban poor to make growth inclusive.
III. Increase manufacturing export share up to 20% of GDP.

Mark the correct code:

Code:

(a) I, II, and III (b) II and III
(c) I and II (d) Only III

7. What is true about industrial performance during post-reform period?

(a) Consistent industrial growth
(b) Higher manufacturing growth
(c) Increase in public sector employment
(d) Decrease in the prices of industrial goods.

8. Which of the following statement(s) is/are not true?

(a) FERA Act, 1973 has been repealed and replaced by FEMA Act, 1999.
(b) Only railway and atomic energy are reserved under public sector.
(c) Industrial licensing is required in the production of drugs and pharmaceuticals.
(d) MOUs signifies an arm's length relationship between government and public sector enterprise.

9. **Which of the following is not the core industry?**
   (a) Textiles (b) Steel
   (c) Coal (d) Cement

10. **What is true about ease of doing business index?**
    I. It is published by World Bank.
    II. It is based on the measurement of 14 sub-indices.
    III. Finland has topped the rankings in 2017, 2018, and 2019.

    Mark the correct code:
    Code:
    (a) I, II and III (b) II and III
    (c) I and III (d) Only I

Chapter 16 Public, Private, and Small Sector in Indian Economy

1. **What is untrue about Maharatna scheme?**
   I. The company eligible for becoming Maharatna should have an average annual turnover of more than ₹20,000 crore during the last 3 years and earn an average annual net worth of more than ₹10,000 crore during the last 3 years.
   II. There are eight Maharatnas notified by the government.
   III. The scheme of Maharatna was launched in the year 1997.

   Mark the correct code:
   Code:
   (a) I and II (b) II and III
   (c) III only (d) I, II, and III

2. **G.V. Ramakrishna commission was established for making suggestions on**
   (a) Disinvestment
   (b) Twin balance sheet problem
   (c) Classification of PSEs
   (d) Dereservation of public sector

3. **How many CPSEs have been granted with Navratna status?**
   (a) 10 (b) 16
   (c) 20 (d) 26

4. **Match the following**

List I	List II
A. Prime Minister's Employment Generation Programme	I. 2008
B. Credit Linked Capital Subsidy Scheme	II. 2000
C. ASPIRE	III. 2005
D. SFURT	IV. 2015

Mark the correct code:

	A	B	C	D
a.	I	II	IV	III
b.	I	II	III	IV
c.	II	III	I	IV
d.	III	I	II	IV

5. **What is true about strategic sales method of disinvestment?**
   I. Government sells shares to a private player along with management.
   II. It is successful in the countries with weak capital market.
   III. The strategic sales have been favorite policy option of the Indian government.

   Mark the correct code:
   Code:
   (a) I and II (b) II and III
   (c) Only I (d) I, II, and III

6. **What is true about insolvency and bankruptcy code (IBC)?**
   I. The code aims to resolve insolvencies in a strict time-bound manner—that is, within 270 days (extendable up to 365 days).
   II. The Insolvency and Bankruptcy Board of India is an apex body for promoting transparency and governance in the administration of the IBC.
   III. National Company Law Tribunal is the adjudicating authority.

   Mark the correct code:
   Code:
   (a) I, II, and III (b) II and III
   (c) I and II (d) Only III

7. What is the definition of medium-scale enterprise in the service sector?

(a) Investment in Plant & Machinery/ Equipment is not more than ₹50 crores & Annual Turnover not more than ₹250 crores.
(b) Investment in Plant & Machinery/ Equipment is not more than ₹5 crores & Annual Turnover not more than ₹50 crores.
(c) Investment in Plant & Machinery/ Equipment is not more than ₹10 crores & Annual Turnover not more than ₹100 crores.
(d) None of the above

8. Which of the following statement(s) is/ are not true?

(a) MSMEs are characterized by decentralized and more inclusive growth than the large corporate sector
(b) As per ET 2018 companies list, Tata Motors is the second largest private corporate in India on a turnover basis
(c) Wrong pricing policy had been the reason for the low efficiency of the public sector
(d) Under the initial public offering, the shares are offered to the public for subscription for the first time along with sale of management

9. Under CSR, all profit-making corporates, including CPSEs are mandated to spend at least ______ of average net profits.

(a) 1% (b) 2%
(c) 3% (d) 4%

10. What is true about twin balance sheet (TBS) problem in India?

I. It was caused by the overheating of Indian economy.
II. In India, TBS coexisted with strong levels of aggregate domestic demand, therefore, did not cause an economic slowdown.
III. IBS code and recapitalization are two plausible routes for resolving TBS problem.

Mark the correct code:

Code:

(a) I, II, and III (b) II and III
(c) I and III (d) Only II

Chapter 17 Service Sector in India—Characteristics, Growth, and Sustainability

1. What is the share of top five services in overall FDI?

(a) 25% (b) 35%
(c) 45% (d) 55%

2. What is the approximate share of services in overall GDP?

(a) 54% (b) 45%
(c) 34% (d) 25%

3. What is the largest item in service exports?

(a) Business service
(b) Financial service
(c) Travel
(d) Software service

4. Match the following

Example	GATS Mode
A. Cross border supply	I. Mode I
B. Consumption abroad	II. Mode II
C. Commercial presence	III. Mode III
D. Presence of a natural person	IV. Mode IV

Mark the correct code:

	A	B	C	D
a.	I	II	III	IV
b.	IV	II	III	I
c.	II	III	I	IV
d.	III	I	II	IV

5. **What is true about service sector?**
   I. Services contribute nearly 80% of GVA and employment, respectively, in both the United States and the United Kingdom.
   II. Services account for more than 70% of global GDP.
   III. As nations grow, their share of services is bound to increase in overall GDP.

   Mark the correct code:

   Code:

   (a) I and II (b) II and III
   (c) Only II (d) I, II and III

6. **Which of the following argument(s) explain(s) the non-sustainability of service sector?**
   I. Employment elasticity of service sector is low
   II. Trade war
   III. A minimum level of educational qualification is pre-requisite to join service sector

   Mark the correct code:

   Code:

   (a) I, II and III (b) II and III
   (c) I and III (d) Only III

7. **What was the approximate share of services as a percentage of GDP at the time of independence?**
   (a) 5% (b) 15%
   (c) 30% (d) 40%

8. **Which of the following factors have contributed into the spectacular growth of service sector in India?**
   I. Increase in per capita income
   II. Increase in service sector exports
   III. The falling productivity in agriculture sector

   Mark the correct code:

   Code:

   (a) I, II and III (b) II and III
   (c) I and II (d) Only III

9. **What is the largest item in service import in India?**
   (a) Software service
   (b) Business service
   (c) Financial service
   (d) Travel

10. **Match the following**

List I	List II
A. Telecommunication	I. Agriculture
B. Electricity	II. Industry
C. Mining	III. Service
D. Poultry	

Mark the correct code:

	A	B	C	D
a.	I	II	III	II
b.	III	II	II	I
c.	II	III	I	III
d.	I	II	III	I

Chapter 18 Foreign Trade and Policy

1. **The FTP 2015–20 notified Visakhapatnam and Bhimavaram in Andhra Pradesh as towns of export excellence in the product category.**
   (a) Shipbuilding
   (b) Seafood
   (c) Gems and jewellery
   (d) Leather products

2. **Which of the following statement(s) is/are true?**
   I. India's total exports have increased by more than 3,000 times and India's total imports have increased by nearly 5,000 times during the last seven decades.
   II. India's share in world exports has declined from 2.2% in 1951 to less than 2% at present.
   III. India's terms of trade vis-à-vis China has deteriorated since 2008.

   Mark the correct code:

   Code:

   (a) I and III (b) II and III
   (c) Only III (d) I, II, and III

3. **Where was Asia's first Export Processing Zone established?**

(a) Ahmedabad (b) Kolkata
(c) Mumbai (d) Kandla

4. **What is not the impact of India's import substitution policy?**

(a) It produced supply side constraints
(b) It discouraged production of luxury goods
(c) It led to generation of unutilized capacity
(d) It led to massive misallocation of resources

5. **Which of the following was/ were the characteristic feature of FTP during pre-reform period?**

I. Export pessimism
II. Import substitution
III. System of managed float

Mark the correct code:

Code:
(a) I and II (b) II and III
(c) Only II (d) I, II, and III

6. **What is true about India's new Foreign Trade Policy 2015–2020?**

I. It aims at increasing the exports of goods and services to $2000 billion by 2019–20.
II. It aims at increasing India's share in world exports to 4.5% by 2019–20.
III. Served from India Scheme has been replaced with Service Exports from India Scheme.

Mark the correct code:

Code:
(a) I, II, and III (b) II and III
(c) I and II (d) Only III

7. **Which is the largest export item of India?**

(a) Gems and jewellery
(b) Machinery and instruments
(c) Readymade garments
(d) Drugs and pharmaceuticals

8. **Which of the following is/are not the disadvantage(s) of SEZ?**

I. Displacement of local inhabitants
II. Regional imbalance
III. More FDI than indigenous investment

Mark the correct code:

Code:
(a) I, II, and III (b) II and III
(c) I and II (d) Only III

9. **What is approximate share of Asia in country's total imports?**

(a) 30% (b) 40%
(c) 50% (d) 60%

10. **Match the following**

List I	List II
A. Special economic zone	I. 1965
B. Export processing zone	II. 2000
C. Export-oriented unit	III. 2001
D. Agriculture export zone	IV. 1981

Mark the correct code:

	A	B	C	D
a.	I	II	III	IV
b.	IV	II	III	I
c.	II	I	IV	III
d.	I	II	IV	III

Chapter 19 Balance of Payments, Foreign Exchange, and Investment

1. **Which of the following statement(s) is/are true?**

I. The current account comprises both goods and services trade.
II. The country experienced current account surplus during three consecutive years 2002–03, 2003–04, and 2004–05.
III. The country experienced a historical high CAD (5.01% of GDP) during 2012–13.

Mark the correct code:

Code:
(a) I and III (b) II and III
(c) III only (d) I only

2. Which of the following statement(s) is/are true regarding Foreign Institutional Investment (FII)?

I. FII is also called hot money.
II. FII is volatile in nature.
III. Tobin tax is suggested on capital flight.

Mark the correct code:

Code:

(a) I and III (b) II and III
(c) Only III (d) I, II, and III

3. Under this mechanism, RBI intervenes in the foreign exchange market to offset the impacts of change in the money supply caused by changes in foreign exchange inflow and outflow. This mechanism is called

(a) Repo Rate (b) Sterilization
(c) Arbitrage (d) Hedging

4. Match the following

List I	List II
A. LERMS	I. 1966
B. System of managed float	II. 1992
C. Devaluation	III. 1993
D. Collapse of Bretton Woods system	IV. 1971

Mark the correct code:

	A	B	C	D
a.	III	II	I	IV
b.	IV	II	III	I
c.	II	III	I	IV
d.	III	I	II	IV

5. Who gave the concept of Purchasing Power Parity?

(a) Gustav Cassel
(b) Milton Friedman
(c) Jagdish Bhagwati
(d) David Hume

6. Which of the following statement(s) is/are true regarding FDI?

I. Delhi NCR is the highest receiver of FDI among all states in India.
II. Singapore is the largest donor of FDI for the last two decades.
III. Service sector is the largest receiver of FDI in the country.

Mark the correct code:

Code:

(a) I, II, and III (b) II and III
(c) I and II (d) Only III

7. Which of the following is the reason for India not adopting Fuller Capital Account Convertibility regime?

(a) Small amount of foreign exchange reserves
(b) High current account deficit
(c) Unstable character of FII
(d) None of the above

8. What is true regarding foreign exchange reserves build up in India during the last two decades?

I. India has a higher stock of foreign exchange reserves than that of China.
II. Invisible receipts have contributed favorably in the foreign exchange reserve build up in the country.
III. FERs in 2017–18 were recorded at more than US$ 500 billion.

Mark the correct code:

Code:

(a) I, II, and III (b) II and III
(c) I and II (d) Only II

9. Which committee gave the new definition of FDI in 2014?

(a) Bimal Jalan Committee
(b) Raghuram Rajan Committee
(c) Y.V. Reddy Committee
(d) Arvind Mayaram Committee

10. Match the following

List I	List II
A. Mexican crisis	I. 1994
B. South Asian crisis	II. 1997
C. Argentina crisis	III. 2001
D. Iceland crisis	IV. 2008

Mark the correct code:

	A	B	C	D
a.	I	II	III	IV
b.	IV	II	III	I
c.	II	III	I	IV
d.	I	II	IV	III

Chapter 20 WTO, International Economic Institutions and Regional Trade Blocks

1. **What is true about TRIPS agreements?**

   I. Under TRIPS agreements process patents are granted for 25 years.
   II. TRIPS agreements encompass seven types of intellectual property rights.
   III. India amended the Patent Act 1970 to make it TRIPS compliant in the year 1995.

   Mark the correct code:

   Code:

   (a) I and II (b) II and III
   (c) II only (d) I, II, and III

2. **Where is headquarter of European Central Bank located?**

   (a) Luxemburg (b) Paris
   (c) Frankfurt (d) Rome

3. **In which ministerial conference decision to remove all export subsidies by 2013 was unanimously taken by WTO members?**

   (a) Doha ministerial conference, 2001
   (b) Hong Kong ministerial conference, 2005
   (c) Bali ministerial conference, 2013
   (d) Cancun ministerial conference, 2003

4. **Match the following**

List I	List II
A. IDA	I. Grants
B. IFC	II. Private Sector
C. MIGA	III. FDI
D. ICSID	IV. Arbitration

   Mark the correct code:

	A	B	C	D
a.	I	II	IV	III
b.	I	II	III	IV
c.	II	IV	III	I
d.	III	I	II	IV

5. **What is true about IMF?**

   I. The headquarter of IMF is located at New York.
   II. India is founding member of IMF.
   III. India is the world's largest borrower of IMF.

   Mark the correct code:

   Code:

   (a) I and II (b) II and III
   (c) Only II (d) I, II, and III

6. **Match the following**

List I	List II
A. OPEC	I. 1999
B. SAARC	II. 1960
C. ASEAN	III. 1967
D. Euro Zone	IV. 1985

   Mark the correct code:

	A	B	C	D
a.	I	II	IV	III
b.	I	II	IV	III
c.	II	IV	III	I
d.	III	I	II	IV

7. **Which of the following statement regarding WTO is true?**

   (a) WTO provides right to impose anti-dumping measures on the discretion of importer nation
   (b) The agreement on Textiles and Clothing expired in 2005 and no longer exists
   (c) Sanitary and phytosanitary measures are in use among member nations as per WHO Good Manufacturer Practices.
   (d) Under the trade policy review mechanism, WTO conducts annual reviews of individual countries' trade policies

8. **Which of the following country is not a member of ASEAN?**

   (a) Cambodia (b) South Korea
   (c) Thailand (d) Philippines

9. **Which of the following statement(s) is/are true?**

   I. India is the largest borrower of World Bank.

II. India became member of World Bank in 1947.

III. The World Bank Group in 2018 endorsed a new Country Partnership Framework (CPF) for India for 2018–2022.

Mark the correct code:

Code:

(a) I and II
(b) I and III
(c) Only I
(d) I, II, and III

10. Match the following

List I	List II
A. Asian Development Bank	I. Beijing
B. UNCTAD	II. Manila
C. Asian Infrastructure Investment Bank	III. Geneva
D. FAO	IV. Rome

Mark the correct code:

	A	B	C	D
a.	I	II	IV	III
b.	I	II	IV	III
c.	II	IV	III	I
d.	II	III	I	IV

Chapter 21 Indian Monetary System: Banking, RBI, and Money Market

1. In which of the cities "minting" of coins is not done?

(a) Mumbai (b) Hyderabad
(c) Noida (d) Bengaluru

2. Consider the following:

I. The scheme of priority sector lending was introduced by RBI in the year 1954.

II. The foreign banks are required to lend 33% of adjusted net bank credit as priority sector lending.

III. The share of agriculture in priority sector lending is 16% of adjusted net bank credit.

Which of the statements given above is/are correct?

(a) I only
(b) II only
(c) Both I and II
(d) None of the above

3. Consider the following statements:

I. The Discount and Finance House in India was established in 1988.

II. Standalone primary dealers function as subsidiaries of banks but not established as non-banking financial corporations.

III. RBI has allowed non-banking financial institutions to accept deposit up to ₹10 lakh.

Which of the statement(s) given above is/are correct?

(a) I only
(b) II only
(c) Both I and II
(d) None of the above

4. Consider the following:

I. M3 is called broad money and is equal to M1+ Time deposits with the banking system.

II. M1 is called narrow money and is equal to currency with the public plus demand deposits with the banking system plus "other" deposits with the RBI.

III. Reserve money is also called "High Powered Money" and is equal to currency in circulation + bankers' deposits with the RBI + "other" deposits with the RBI.

Which of the above is/are true?

(a) I only (b) II and III only
(c) II and III only (d) I, II, and III

5. Which of the following is the incorrect statement?

(a) Imperial bank of India was converted into Sate bank of India in 1955
(b) The small finance bank is a private financial institution

(c) A payment bank can accept demand deposits up to ₹1 lakh
(d) Local area banks are public sector banks having jurisdiction over two or three contiguous districts

6. Match the following:

List I	List II
A. Sterilization	I. Injecting short-term liquidity by RBI
B. Repo rate	II. RBI intervention in foreign exchange market
C. Bank rate	III. Rediscounting of bills of exchange by RBI
D. Marginal standing facility	IV. Lending by RBI in emergency situation

Mark the correct code:

	A	B	C	D
a.	II	I	IV	III
b.	I	II	III	IV
c.	II	IV	III	I
d.	II	I	III	IV

7. Consider the following:

I. An asset will be considered NPA for which the principal or interest payment remained overdue for a period of 60 days.
II. Ever-greening signifies fresh loans given to company to enable it to pay off its interest.
III. In India, majority of NPAs constitute lending by private sector banks.

Which of the above is/are true?

(a) II only (b) I and III only
(c) II and III only (d) I, II, and III

8. In which year Lead Bank Scheme was introduced in India?

(a) 1969 (b) 1977
(c) 1981 (d) 1988

9. Match the following:

List I	List II
A. Payment banks	I. Y.V. Reddy
B. Lead Banks	II. F.K.F. Nariman
C. Commercial papers	III. Nachiket Mor
D. Liquidity aggregates	IV. N. Vaghul

Mark the correct code:

	A	B	C	D
a.	II	I	IV	III
b.	I	II	III	IV
c.	II	IV	III	I
d.	III	II	IV	I

10. Which of the following can be considered as banking sector reform measure?

(a) Pradhan mantra Jan Dhan Yojana
(b) Priority sector lending
(c) Banking Ombudsman Scheme
(d) None of the above

Chapter 22 Indian Capital Market

1. TOPIX is the popular share price index of ______.

(a) New York Stock Exchange
(b) London Stock Exchange
(c) Japan Exchange Group
(d) Shanghai Stock Exchange

2. What is gilt-edged market?

(a) It is market for government securities
(b) The market where shares of blue chip companies are bought and sold
(c) The market where shares of foreign MNCs are traded
(d) None of the above

3. Consider the following statements:

I. NSE was established in Mumbai in 1992.
II. NSE was established on the recommendation of Narasimham Committee.
III. NSE is the largest stock exchange in India in terms of total and average daily turnover for equity shares.

Which of the statements given above is/are correct?

(a) I only (b) II only
(c) Both I and III (d) None of the above

4. Consider the following:

I. Sensex was launched in 1988.
II. The base period of Sensex is 2011–2012.
III. Sensex is calculated using the weighted average market capitalization method.

Which of the above statement(s) is/are true?

(a) I only
(b) I and III only
(c) II and III only
(d) None of the above

5. In which year Calcutta Stock Exchange was established?

(a) 1893 (b) 1908
(c) 1914 (d) 1928

6. Match the following:

List I	List II
A. UTI	I. 1990
B. NHB	II. 1987
C. SIDBI	III. 1956
D. LIC	IV. 1964

Mark the correct code:

	A	B	C	D
a.	II	I	IV	III
b.	IV	II	I	III
c.	II	IV	III	I
d.	III	I	II	IV

7. What is true about Bombay Stock Exchange (BSE)?

(a) It is Asia's second oldest stock exchange.
(b) It was corporatized in 1991.
(c) Equity Derivatives were introduced in 2005.
(d) It is India's first Universal Exchange.

8. In which year SEBI was provided with statutory powers?

(a) 1988 (b) 1992
(c) 1997 (d) 2001

9. Match the following:

List I	List II
A. Satyam Scam	I. Jignesh Shah
B. NSEL Scam	II. Nirav Modi
C. Saradha Scam	III. Ramalinga Raju
D. Punjab National Bank Scam	IV. Sudipto Sen

Mark the correct code:

	A	B	C	D
a.	II	I	IV	III
b.	I	II	III	IV
c.	II	IV	III	I
d.	III	I	IV	II

10. In which year Industrial Finance Corporation of India (IFCI) was established?

(a) 1948 (b) 1969
(c) 1982 (d) 1988

Chapter 23 Inflation in India

1. What is true about Consumer Price Index (CPI) combined?

I. Food and beverages constitute more than 50% weight in CPI basket.
II. The number of items in CPI basket is 299.
III. RBI uses CPI as an indicator of inflation for its monetary policy.

Mark the correct code:

Code:

(a) I and II (b) II and III
(c) II only (d) I, II, and III

2. What is the number of items in the WPI with new series 2011–2012?

(a) 674 (b) 697
(c) 714 (d) 754

3. **Who calculates Wholesale Price Index in India?**
   (a) Department of Industrial policy and Promotion, Ministry of Commerce and Industry
   (b) Department of Economic affairs, Ministry of Finance
   (c) Central Statistical Office
   (d) National Sample Survey Office

4. **Which of the following can be regarded the demand side factor(s) of inflation?**
   I. Higher GDP growth
   II. Rise in administered prices
   III. Black Money

   Mark the correct code:
   Code:
   (a) I and II
   (b) I and III
   (c) Only II
   (d) I, II, and III

5. **Match the following:**

List I	List II
A. CPI Combined	I. 2012
B. CPI-AL	II. 2000–2001
C. CPI-RL	III. 1986–1987
D. CPI-IW	

Mark the correct code:

	A	B	C	D
a.	I	II	II	III
b.	I	II	I	III
c.	I	III	III	II
d.	III	I	I	II

6. **Who headed the Expert Committee to Revise and Strengthen the Monetary Policy Framework in 2013?**
   (a) Raghuram Rajan
   (b) Urjit Patel
   (c) C. Rangarajan
   (d) Shaktikanta Das

7. **What should not be the plausible reason for increase in prices?**
   (a) Rise in Sensex
   (b) Devaluation of rupee
   (c) Increase in global oil prices
   (d) None of the above

8. **Which of the following statement(s) is/are true?**
   I. The core inflation is arrived by excluding food and fuel inflation from total inflation.
   II. CPI (Agriculture Labour and Rural Labour) is compiled and released by CSO.
   III. In hyper-inflation, prices rise every moment, and there is no limit to the height to which prices might rise.

   Mark the correct code:
   Code:
   (a) I and II (b) I and III
   (c) Only I (d) I, II, and III

9. **Match the following:**

List I	List II
A. Retail Inflation	I. CPI
B. Protein Inflation	II. Food items
C. Core inflation	III. Manufacturing
D. Headline Inflation	IV. All products

Mark the correct code:

	A	B	C	D
a.	I	II	III	IV
b.	I	II	IV	III
c.	III	I	II	IV
d.	III	IV	II	I

10. **Which of the following measure(s) can help arresting prices in a country?**
    (a) Dear money policy
    (b) Reduction in import duty
    (c) Restricting exports
    (d) All of the above

Chapter 24 Indian Tax System

1. Laffer curve describes

(a) Tax elasticity (b) Tax buoyancy
(c) Tax equity (d) All of the above

2. Which of the following statement is incorrect?

(a) Long-term capital gain tax is payable at 10% on profit exceeding ₹1 lakh made from the sale of shares or equity mutual fund schemes held for over 1 year
(b) Minimum alternate tax is levied at the rate of 15% of the book profits (plus surcharge and cess as applicable)
(c) Securities Transaction Tax is charged at the rate of 0.1% of share value on buying and selling of equity shares
(d) Government of India introduced "donor-based" gift tax in the year 2005

3. Consider the following statements:

I. There are five GST tax slabs apart from exempt category of 0%.
II. GST is a source-based consumption tax.
III. Under GST, tax on sale and purchase of newspapers is charged at 5%.

Which of the statement(s) given above is/are correct?

(a) I only
(b) II only
(c) Both I and II
(d) None of the above

4. Consider the following:

I. Fringe Benefit Tax
II. Long-term capital gain tax
III. Securities Transaction Tax

Which of the above is/are Direct Tax/Taxes?

(a) I only (b) I and III only
(c) II and III only (d) I, II, and III

5. Which one of the following is the correct statement?

(a) GST rates in India are among the highest in the world.
(b) An example of specific tax in India is custom duty.
(c) Land revenue cannot be levied by state government after the implementation of GST.
(d) All of the above

6. Match the following

List I	List II
A. Raja J. Chelliah Committee	I. GST model
B. Asim Dasgupta Committee	II. Tax evasion and black money
C. Wanchoo Committee	III. Direct and indirect tax reforms
D. Kaldor Committee	IV. Wealth tax

Mark the correct code:

	A	B	C	D
a.	II	I	IV	III
b.	I	II	III	IV
c.	II	IV	III	I
d.	III	I	I	IV

7. Agricultural income tax is assigned to the state government by

(a) the Finance Commission
(b) the National Development Council
(c) the Inter-State Council
(d) the Constitution of India

8. Which of the following tax/taxes is/are collected by Panchayat?

(a) VAT (b) Land revenue
(c) Professional (d) All of the above

9. Match the following

List I	List II
A. Wealth Tax	I. 1994
B. Service tax	II. 1957
C. VAT	III. 2004
D. Securities Transaction Tax	IV. 2005

Mark the correct code:

	A	B	C	D
a.	II	I	IV	III
b.	I	II	III	IV
c.	II	IV	III	I
d.	III	I	I	IV

10. Which committee is credited with the construction of GST model of India?

(a) Asim Dasgupta Committee
(b) Vijay Kelkar Committee
(c) C. Rangarajan Committee
(d) None of the above

Chapter 25 Public Expenditure, Debt Management, and Fiscal Policy

1. Which of the following will have positive impact on the fiscal health of Indian economy?

I. Increase in debt service ratio
II. Increase in the maturity period of debt
III. Declining ratio of interest payments to revenue receipts

Mark the correct code:

Code:
(a) I and III (b) II and III
(c) I, II, and III (d) I only

2. Which of the following statement(s) is/are true?

I. The share of subsidies as a proportion of total GDP is less than 2.5%.
II. Fertilizer and pesticide subsidies are the example of perverse subsidies.
III. In India, the share of explicit subsidies is greater than that of implicit subsidies.

Mark the correct code:

Code:
(a) I and II (b) II and III
(c) Only III (d) I, II, and III

3. In which year inflation-indexed bonds were introduced in India?

(a) 1999 (b) 2005
(c) 2013 (d) 2017

4. Match the following

List I	List II
A. Free LPG connection to poor	I. Demerit good
B. Construction of park	II. Merit good
C. Free electricity to farmers	III. Public good
D. Subsidizing primary education	

Mark the correct code:

	A	B	C	D
a.	I	II	III	III
b.	I	II	III	I
c.	II	III	I	II
d.	III	I	II	II

5. State provident fund is the part of

I. public debt
II. other liabilities
III. domestic debt

Mark the correct code:

Code:
(a) I and II
(b) II and III
(c) Only II
(d) I, II, and III

6. Which of the following is the capital expenditure in Government of India's budget?

I. Subsidies
II. Construction of dams
III. Grants-in-aid to states

Mark the correct code:

Code:
(a) I, II, and III
(b) II and III
(c) I and II
(d) Only II

7. **Match the following**

List I	List II
A. High Level Expert Committee on Efficient Management of Public Expenditure	I. C. Rangarajan
B. Expenditure Management Commission	II. Bimal Jalan
C. Expenditure reform commission	III. K.P. Geetha Krishnan
D. FRBM Act review committee	III. N.K. Singh

Mark the correct code:

	A	B	C	D
a.	II	I	III	IV
b.	IV	II	III	I
c.	II	III	I	IV
d.	I	II	III	IV

8. **Which of the following is not the recommendation made by N.K. Singh Committee on reviewing the FRBM Act?**
   I. A debt to GDP ratio of 60% should be targeted with a 35% limit for the center and 15% limit for the states and the targets should be achieved by 2023.
   II. An autonomous Fiscal Council must be created with a chairperson and two members appointed by the center.
   III. The government may be allowed to deviate from the specified targets by not more than 1% of GDP in a year.

   Mark the correct code:
   Code:
   (a) I, II, and III (b) II and III
   (c) I and III (d) Only III

9. **What is the approximate share of external debt as a percentage of GDP?**
   (a) <5% (b) 5–10%
   (c) 20–25% (d) 30–35%

10. **Match the following**

List I	List II
A. Fiscal deficit	I. Interest payments
B. Primary deficit	II. Borrowings
C. Effective revenue deficit	III. Grants-in-aid to states
D. Budgetary deficit	IV. Total expenditure and receipts

Mark the correct code:

	A	B	C	D
a.	II	I	III	IV
b.	IV	II	III	I
c.	II	III	I	IV
d.	I	II	IV	III

Chapter 26 Center–State Financial Relations in India

1. **What is true about finance commission?**
   (a) There have been 15 commissions till date, and so far 14 commissions have submitted their report
   (b) The first Finance Commission was established by the President of India in 1952
   (c) Prime minister is the ex officio chairman of FC
   (d) The term of Finance Commission is 6 years

2. **The allocation between the states of the respective shares of union transfers is called**
   (a) divisible pool
   (b) vertical devolution
   (c) horizontal devolution
   (d) none of the above

3. **What is untrue about 14th finance commission?**
   (a) the share of states has been raised from 32 to 42% of divisible pool;
   (b) in the horizontal devolution formula two new variables-population and fiscal discipline have been incorporated;
   (c) the income distance has been given the weight of 50%; and

(d) fiscal deficit of all states will be affixed to an annual limit of 3% of GSDP.

4. Under 14th finance commission, the state with highest share of tax devolution is

(a) Bihar
(b) Andhra Pradesh
(c) Uttar Pradesh
(d) Jammu and Kashmir

5. Who is the chairman of 15th finance commission?

(a) Y.V. Reddy (b) N.K. Singh
(c) Urjit Patel (d) C. Rangarajan

6. What is not true about special category states?

(a) 5th Finance Commission introduced the concept of a special category state in the year 1969;
(b) Andhra Pradesh is not a special category state;
(c) such states get special financial assistance from the central government; and
(d) such states are characterized by higher population density and poverty.

7. Consider the following statements and select the correct code given below

I. Article 243 (I) prescribes State Finance Commission for Panchayats and Article 243 (Y) prescribes State Finance Commission for municipalities.
II. State Finance Commission is required to review the financial position of the local bodies and make recommendations to the Chief Minister.
III. The State Finance Commission was created by the 73rd and 74th Constitutional (Amendment) Acts.

Code:

(a) I and II (b) I and III
(c) I, II, and III (d) II and III

8. In India vertical and horizontal imbalances have emerged because of

I. excessive pressure on states due to fiscal discipline;
II. decline in grants to states; and
III. undue weightage given to certain variables like population.

Select the correct statement using the code given below:

(a) I and II (b) I and III
(c) I, II, and III (d) II and III

9. Which of the following is not the principal of fiscal federalism?

(a) efficiency and economy
(b) fiscal equalization
(c) progressive taxation
(d) adequacy and elasticity

10. Mark the incorrect statement.

(a) Fiscal discipline is the ability of the state to generate revenue
(b) Article 275 of the constitution prescribes states to provide for grants-in-aid to the states
(c) Gadgil formula was given by D. R. Gadgil in the year 1969
(d) 15th Finance Commission is required to make recommendation for the period 2020–2025

Chapter 27 Planning in India

1. Who among the following formulated "People's plan"?

(a) Shriman Narayan
(b) M.N. Roy
(c) M. Visvervaraya
(d) S.N. Agarwala

2. Which of the following can be attributed as failure of planning in India?

I. Modest growth rate during initial years of planning failed to redistribute income in favor of marginalized section of society.
II. Emphasis on growth rather than on employment and the adoption of capital-intensive production techniques is widely held responsible for the continuous increase of unemployment in India.
III. Indian economy failed to emerge as competitive and productive vis-à-vis other emerging markets.

Mark the correct code:

Code:

(a) I and II (b) I and III
(c) Only I (d) I, II, and III

3. **Which of the following statement is false?**
   (a) Achieved growth rate was less than targeted growth rate during most of the plans.
   (b) First five-year plan was based on Harrod–Domar model.
   (c) The famous "Garibi hatao" slogan was given during fifth five-year plan.
   (d) The main theme of 12th five-year plan was "faster, more inclusive, and sustainable growth."

4. **Which of the following statement(s) regarding Planning Commission and NITI Aayog is/are true?**
   I. Planning Commission enjoyed power to allocate funds but NITI Aayog does not.
   II. NITI Aayog is more centralized and enjoys more discretionary powers than Planning Commission.
   III. Planning Commission had full-time members but NITI Aayog has only part-time members.

Mark the correct code:

Code:

(a) I and II
(b) I and III
(c) Only I
(d) I, II, and III

5. **Match the following**

List I	List II
A. National Planning Committee	I. G.D. Birla
B. Planned economy for India	II. M. Visvervaraya
C. Bombay Plan	III. Jawahar Lal Nehru
D. Gandhian Plan	IV. Shriman Narayan

Mark the correct code:

	A	B	C	D
a.	I	II	II	III
b.	I	II	I	III
c.	I	III	III	II
d.	III	II	I	IV

6. **In which five-year plan India adopted indicative planning?**
   (a) Second five-year plan
   (b) Fifth five-year plan
   (c) Sixth five-year plan
   (d) Eighth five-year plan

7. **In which year rolling plan was introduced in India?**
   (a) 1972–73 (b) 1977–78
   (c) 1980–81 (d) 1990–91

8. **What is true about NITI Aayog's comprehensive national Strategy for New India?**
   I. Accelerating the economy to achieve a GDP growth rate of about 8% on average to make it $4 trillion economy by 2030.
   II. Establishing at least 10,000 Atal Tinkering Labs by 2020.
   III. Raising the export of goods and services to $800 billion a year by 2022–23, as against the $478 billion in 2018.

Mark the correct code:

Code:

(a) I and II (b) II and III
(c) Only I (d) I, II, and III

9. **Which five-year plan marked the beginning of economic liberalization in India?**
   (a) Sixth five-year plan
   (b) Seventh five-year plan
   (c) Eighth five-year plan
   (d) Ninth five-year plan

10. **Which of the following is/are not the function(s) of NITI Aayog?**
    (a) To foster cooperative federalism
    (b) To promote innovation
    (c) To allocate funds in the productive sectors of the economy
    (d) To actively monitor and evaluate the implementation of programs and initiatives

Chapter 28 Black Money and Demonetization

1. What are the objectives of demonetization?

I. to check counterfeiting
II. to control hyperinflation
III. to discourage terrorist activities

Mark the correct code:

Code:

(a) I and II
(b) I and III
(c) I, II, and III
(d) II and III

2. Which of the following is/are the consequence(s) of black money?

I. Inflation
II. Conspicuous consumption
III. Investment in real estate

Mark the correct code:

Code:

(a) I and III
(b) II and III
(c) Only III
(d) I, II, and III

3. Which factor is not responsible for the generation of black money?

(a) Counterfeiting
(b) Inflation
(c) Money Laundering
(d) Laissez Faire

4. Match the following:

List I	List II
A. VDIS	I. 1997
B. IDS	II. 2016
C. RTI Act	III. 2005
D. The Prevention of Money Laundering Act	IV. 2002

Mark the correct code:

	A	B	C	D
a.	I	II	III	IV
b.	II	I	IV	III
c.	II	III	I	IV
d.	III	I	II	IV

5. Match the following:

List I	List II
A. Pakistan	I. 2013
B. Zimbabwe	II. 2016
C. Venezuela	III. 2015
D. Cyprus	

Mark the correct code:

	A	B	C	D
a.	I	II	III	II
b.	II	I	I	III
c.	III	III	I	II
d.	III	III	II	I

6. What is true about money laundering?

I. It is the act of making money that comes from Source A looks like it comes from Source B.
II. Layering refers to the reinjection of the laundered proceeds back into the economy.
III. The Prevention of Money Laundering Act (PMLA), 2002 was enacted to prevent and control money laundering.

Mark the correct code:

Code:

(a) I, II, and III
(b) II and III
(c) I and III
(d) Only II

7. When was demonetization first introduced in independent India?

(a) 1948 (b) 1978
(c) 1991 (d) 2016

8. Match the following:

List I	List II
A. Wanchoo Committee	I. 1974
B. Venkatappaiah Committee	II. 1969
C. Kelkar committee	III. 2002
D. Chelliah Committee	IV. 1993

Mark the correct code:

	A	B	C	D
a.	I	II	III	IV
b.	II	I	IV	III
c.	II	I	III	IV
d.	III	I	II	IV

9. What is the rank of India as per corruption perceptions index (CPI) 2018?

(a) 131 (b) 92
(c) 78 (d) 110

10. What is true about black money estimations outside India?

I. Black money outside India generally takes place through mis-invoicing and takes the shape of round tripping as well.
II. According to a study by US-based think-tank Global Financial Integrity (GFI), more than $700 billion in black money entered India during 2005–2014.
III. The amount of black money lying outside India is far greater than that of within the country.

Mark the correct code:

Code:

(a) I, II, and III (b) I and II
(c) Only I (d) II and III

Chapter 29 Economic Reforms in India

1. Who coined the term Washington consensus?

(a) Jagdish Bhagwati
(b) Raghuram Rajan
(c) John Williamson
(d) Philippe Le Houerou

2. Match the following:

List I	List II
A. IRDA	I. 1999
B. TRAI	II. 1997
C. SEBI	III. 1992
D. NSE	

Mark the correct code:

	A	B	C	D
a.	I	II	III	III
b.	III	II	II	I
c.	II	III	I	III
d.	I	III	II	I

3. Financial market reforms in India did not include

(a) Establishment of SEBI
(b) Establishment of IRDA
(c) Establishment of TRAI
(d) Establishment of NSE

4. Consider the following statements:

I. Dr Manmohan Singh is hailed as father of economic reforms in India.
II. Rupee was devalued in the year 1993.
III. Washington consensus contained a set of 10 economic policy prescriptions for crisis-wracked developing countries.

Mark the correct code:

Code:

(a) Only 1 (b) I and II
(c) Only III (d) I, II, and III

5. Which factor(s) was/were responsible for the economic crisis of 1990?

I. Higher fiscal deficit
II. Unstable political environment
III. Oil crisis

Mark the correct code:

Code:

(a) Only 1 (b) I and II
(c) Only III (d) I, II, and III

6. Which of the following argument(s) explain(s) the negative consequence of India's economic reforms?

I. Jobless growth
II. Widening of income inequalities
III. Red tape

Mark the correct code:

Code:

(a) I, II, and III (b) II and III
(c) I and II (d) Only III

7. Which of the following argument(s) explain(s) the positive consequence of India's economic reforms?

I. Higher growth rate
II. Increase in India's export share
III. Current account surplus

Mark the correct code:

Code:

(a) I, II, and III (b) II and III
(c) Only I (d) Only III

8. What reformative steps were undertaken to correct balance of payment crisis of 1991?

I. Adoption of managed float exchange rate system
II. Devaluation of rupee
III. Reduction in peak rate of custom duty

Mark the correct code:

Code:

(a) I, II, and III (b) II and III
(c) I and II (d) Only III

9. Which of the following is the component of structural adjustment reforms?

(a) Fiscal policy reforms
(b) Tax reforms
(c) Agriculture reforms
(d) Balance of payment reforms

10. Match the following:

List I	List II
A. Tax reforms	I. Liberalization
B. WTO	II. Privatization
C. Disinvestment	III. Globalization
D. Deregulation of interest rate	

Mark the correct code:

	A	B	C	D
a.	I	II	III	II
b.	III	II	II	I
c.	II	III	I	III
d.	I	III	II	I

ANSWER KEYS TO MCQs

Chapter 1
1. c 2. b 3. a 4. a 5. d 6. a 7. c 8. d 9. a 10. c

Chapter 2
1. a 2. b 3. d 4. d 5. d 6. b 7. c 8. d 9. a 10. c

Chapter 3
1. a 2. b 3. c 4. c 5. d 6. d 7. d 8. a 9. c 10. d

Chapter 4
1. b 2. d 3. a 4. a 5. d 6. b 7. b 8. a 9. c 10. c

Chapter 5
1. d 2. a 3. b 4. b 5. d 6. d 7. b 8. a 9. c 10. d

Chapter 6
1. a 2. d 3. c 4. d 5. a 6. a 7. c 8. a 9. a 10. b

Chapter 7
1. d 2. a 3. a 4. d 5. c 6. c 7. b 8. b 9. b 10. d

Chapter 8
1. a 2. b 3. d 4. c 5. d 6. c 7. b 8. b 9. b 10. d

Chapter 9
1. c 2. c 3. b 4. a 5. c 6. d 7. c 8. c 9. c 10. c

Chapter 10
1. d 2. a 3. a 4. b 5. a 6. d 7. b 8. a 9. d 10. a

Chapter 11
1. a 2. d 3. b 4. a 5. c 6. c 7. d 8. a 9. b 10. d

Chapter 12
1. a 2. c 3. c 4. d 5. d 6. d 7. d 8. a 9. c 10. c

Chapter 13
1. c 2. d 3. d 4. c 5. a 6. d 7. a 8. d 9. a 10. a

Chapter 14
1. d 2. d 3. d 4. b 5. d 6. a 7. b 8. d 9. a 10. c

Chapter 15
1. d 2. b 3. b 4. a 5. c 6. d 7. b 8. c 9. a 10. d

Chapter 16

1. a **2.** a **3.** b **4.** a **5.** a **6.** b **7.** a **8.** d **9.** b **10.** a

Chapter 17

1. c **2.** a **3.** d **4.** a **5.** d **6.** c **7.** c **8.** c **9.** b **10.** b

Chapter 18

1. b **2.** d **3.** d **4.** b **5.** a **6.** d **7.** a **8.** d **9.** d **10.** c

Chapter 19

1. a **2.** d **3.** b **4.** c **5.** a **6.** d **7.** c **8.** d **9.** d **10.** a

Chapter 20

1. c **2.** c **3.** b **4.** b **5.** c **6.** c **7.** b **8.** b **9.** b **10.** d

Chapter 21

1. d **2.** d **3.** a **4.** d **5.** d **6.** d **7.** a **8.** a **9.** d **10.** c

Chapter 22

1. c **2.** a **3.** c **4.** d **5.** b **6.** b **7.** d **8.** b **9.** d **10.** a

Chapter 23

1. b **2.** b **3.** a **4.** b **5.** c **6.** b **7.** a **8.** b **9.** a **10.** d

Chapter 24

1. a **2.** d **3.** d **4.** d **5.** a **6.** d **7.** d **8.** c **9.** a **10.** a

Chapter 25

1. b **2.** a **3.** c **4.** c **5.** b **6.** d **7.** d **8.** c **9.** a **10.** a

Chapter 26

1. a **2.** c **3.** b **4.** c **5.** b **6.** d **7.** b **8.** c **9.** c **10.** a

Chapter 27

1. b **2.** d **3.** c **4.** c **5.** d **6.** d **7.** b **8.** b **9.** a **10.** c

Chapter 28

1. c **2.** d **3.** d **4.** a **5.** d **6.** c **7.** b **8.** c **9.** c **10.** b

Chapter 29

1. c **2.** a **3.** c **4.** c **5.** d **6.** c **7.** c **8.** a **9.** c **10.** d

Notes

Notes